Life in the United Kingdom
Official Study Guide

Jenny Wales

part of Williams Lea Tag

Published by TSO (The Stationery Office), part of Williams Lea Tag, and available from:

Online
www.tsoshop.co.uk

Mail, Telephone, Fax & E-mail
TSO
PO Box 29, Norwich, NR3 1GN
Telephone orders/General enquiries: 0333 202 5070
Fax orders: 0333 202 5080
E-mail: customer.services@tso.co.uk
Textphone 0333 202 5077

TSO@Blackwell and other Accredited Agents

The information contained in this publication is believed to be correct at the time of manufacture. Whilst care has been taken to ensure that the information is accurate, the publisher can accept no responsibility for any errors or omissions or for changes to the details given.

ISBN 9780113413423

Ninth impression 2017

Printed in the United Kingdom

Contents

Acknowledgments

Practice questions by Michael Mitchell.

This publication has been approved by the Home Office.

Photographic credits

Page 10
Campus Life/Getty Images

Page 14
Robert Nicholas/Getty Images

Page 36
View Pictures/Universal Images Group/
Getty Images

Page 41
Hulton Archive/Getty Images

Page 44
Apic/Hulton Fine Art Collection/Getty Images

Page 49
Studio of Sir Peter Lely/Getty Images

Page 55
Science & Society Picture Library/Getty Images

Page 57
Globe Turner/Getty Images

Page 61
Bob Thomas/Popperfoto/Getty Images

Page 63
Steve Allen/Getty Images

Page 66
Central Press/Hulton Archive/Getty Images

Page 68
Edward G Malindine/Hulton Archive/
Getty Images

Page 86
Bob Wickham/Getty Images

Page 95
Jeff J Mitchell/Getty Images

Page 97
Queen's House, Greenwich: Mike Marlow/
Gallo Images/Getty Images
St Paul's Cathedral: John Harper/Getty Images
Dumfries House: Helena Smith/Getty Images
Harewood House: David Else/Getty Images
Houses of Parliament: Scott E Barbour/
Getty Images
St Pancras Station: Buena Vista Images/
Getty Images

Cenotaph: David Clapp/Getty Images
30 St Mary Axe: Michael Blann/Digital Vision/
Getty Images

Page 101
The Eden Project: Fergus Kennedy/
Getty Images
Edinburgh Castle: Ary Diesendruck/
Getty Images
The Giant's Causeway: Slow Images/
Getty Images
Loch Lomond: Adam Burton/Getty Images
London Eye: Guy Vanderelst/Getty Images
Snowdonia: Loraine Wilson/Getty Images
The Tower of London: Image Source/
Getty Images
The Lake District: Environment Images/
Universal Images Group/Getty Images

Page 114
Scott E Barbour/Getty Images

Page 115
Universal Images Group/Getty Images

Page 116
Alain Benainous/Gamma-Rapho/
Getty Images

Page 124
Fuse/Getty Images

Introduction:
the Life in the UK test

Preparing for the Life in the UK test

What do I need to learn for the Life in the UK test?

To pass the Life in the UK test, you need to read and understand ALL chapters in *Life in the United Kingdom: A Guide for New Residents* (3rd edition). The chapters cover a range of topics you will need to know as a permanent resident or citizen of the UK:

- The values and principles of the UK
- The countries that make up the UK
- The events and people that have shaped our history
- Aspects of life in the UK
- How our country is governed
- How you can get involved in your community

How should I use this guide?

This guide is designed to be used with *Life in the United Kingdom: A Guide for New Residents*.

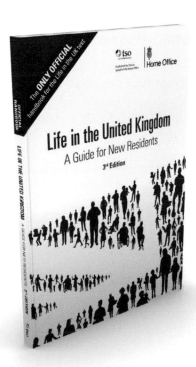

It offers a summary of the content and helps you to learn the material that you need to understand for the Life in the UK test. At the beginning of each chapter you will find a chart or diagram which shows an outline of the key information you will need to learn.

Throughout the text there are 'Find out' boxes like the one below. To give a full answer to the questions you will need to refer to *Life in the United Kingdom: A Guide for New Residents.*

Find out ...

✓ Why did the First World War happen?

✓ Which countries were involved in the First World War?

At the end of each chapter there are questions drawn from the ones you might be asked when you take the test.

What does the test involve?

You will be asked 24 different questions. There are four types of question in the test.

The first type of question involves **selecting one correct answer from four options**. Here is an example of this type of question.

> Where is the UK Parliament based?
>
> ☐ **A** Holyrood
> ☐ **B** Senedd
> ☐ **C** Stormont
> ☐ **D** Westminster
>
> (The correct answer is D.)

The second type of question involves **deciding whether a statement is true or false**. Here is an example of this second type of question.

Is the statement below ☐ TRUE or ☐ FALSE?

> 'The Battle of Britain' was an aerial battle against the Germans during the Second World War.

(The correct answer is TRUE.)

The third type of question involves **selecting the statement which you think is correct** from a choice of two statements. Here is an example of this third type of question.

Which of the following statements is correct?

☐ **A** The thistle is the national flower of Scotland.

☐ **B** The daffodil is the national flower of Scotland.

(The correct answer is A.)

The final type of question involves **selecting two correct answers from four options**. You need to select **both** correct answers to get a point on this type of question. Here is an example of this fourth type of question.

Which TWO are famous British artists?

☐ **A** Thomas Gainsborough

☐ **B** Sir John Lavery

☐ **C** Benjamin Britten

☐ **D** Graham Greene

(The correct answer is A and B.)

You can also use *Life in the United Kingdom: Official Practice Questions and Answers* to help you practise for the test. It contains more than 400 practice questions and answers, plus explanations for each question. For more information about this publication, visit: www.tsoshop.co.uk/LIFE

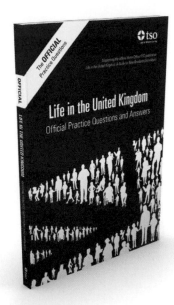

What level of English do I need to take the test?

The questions in the Life in the UK test are written at a level of English equivalent to English for Speakers of Other Languages (ESOL) Entry Level 3. The English language requirements for permanent residence or citizenship may change from time to time. You can check the current requirements on the UK Border Agency website at:

www.ukba.homeoffice.gov.uk

How can I study for the test?

Here are a few techniques which might help you to study.

When to study

- Plan in advance when you are going to study – make yourself a timetable and give yourself enough time before your test date to learn the information you need to know. Make sure you have a quiet place where you can study.

- Study for short periods and have a break regularly. If you get tired, it will be hard to concentrate.
- If there is nowhere quiet where you live, the local library may be a good place to study.

Check your understanding

- After reading each section, ask yourself 'What was the main point?' If you can describe it to yourself in your own words, then you have understood and you are more likely to remember it and to be able to answer questions about it.
- The 'Find out' questions aim to help you learn. They mainly refer to content in the handbook, *Life in the United Kingdom: A Guide for New Residents*, so they test your full understanding. When you have gone through each short part of the study guide, test yourself on the 'Find out' questions and check back to the handbook to see if you have the right answer. The content of the two publications is in the same order, so the answers are easy to find.

Make notes

- Have a pencil or pen and some small pieces of paper or index cards available on which you can make notes.
- After reading each section, decide what the main points are and write the important facts onto the pieces of paper or index cards. Do not write too much, as you need to be able to scan the facts easily.

Practice questions

- When you have finished each chapter, complete the practice questions in this guide. If you find that you have got something wrong, the answers section will point you to the section of *Life in the United Kingdom: A Guide for New Residents* which you need to go back to and read again.

Revision

- Whenever you have a spare moment, read through some of your notes, or stick them on the wall somewhere in your home and look at them regularly. Reviewing your notes often will help you to remember the information.

- It might help to study with a friend who is also taking the test. You can discuss parts of the guide that were difficult to understand and test each other's knowledge.

If you find revision difficult, ask a friend or family member to test you on the information in your notes or directly from the guide.

Taking the test

How do I book a test?

You can only book your test online at:

www.lituktestbooking.co.uk

You cannot book the test by post or by any other means. You should not take your test at any other establishment, as the UK Border Agency will only accept certificates from registered test centres.

The earliest you can take a test is seven days from the date of booking.

Where can I take the test?

You can only take the test at a registered and approved Life in the UK test centre. There are about 60 test centres around the UK. You will be given details of your nearest test centre when you book.

How much will the test cost and how do I pay for it?

The test costs £50. You must pay this online with a debit or credit card when you book your test.

Do I need to bring any identification to the test centre?

You **must** bring photographic identification (ID) with you to the test centre to show to the test supervisor. You will **not** be allowed to take the test without your photographic ID.

You must bring one of the following forms of ID:

- a passport from your country of origin
- a UK photocard driving licence, full or provisional
- one of the following Home Office travel documents:
  - a Convention Travel Document (CTD)
  - a Certificate of Identity Document (CID)
  - a Stateless Person Document (SPD)
- a European Union identity card
- an Immigration Status Document, endorsed with a UK residence permit and bearing a photo of the holder (which must be together on the same document)
- a biometric residence permit.

You will also need to bring proof of your postcode. This should be an original (not a photocopy) of one of the following documents:

- gas, electricity or water bill
- Council Tax bill
- bank or credit card statement
- UK photocard driving licence (this can also be used as photographic ID)
- letter from the Home Office with your name and address on it.

The documents you can use may change in the future. You should check the UK Border Agency website for up-to-date information at www.ukba.homeoffice.gov.uk.

What facilities are there for people with disabilities?

You will be asked about your needs when you book your test. The test centre will make the necessary arrangements to give you the support you need so you can complete the test.

How do I take the test?

You take the test using a computer. You will have 45 minutes to do the test. This gives you plenty of time to choose your answers and check them again before the end. You do not need to rush to finish the test quickly. Use all of the time that you are given. Headphones are available for you to listen to the questions and answer options.

What happens on the day of the test?

When you arrive at the test centre, you will need to present the supervisor with the ID you registered with and a document showing proof of your postcode. You won't be able to take your test if you don't have these documents with you.

The supervisor will check your documents and, once verified, you will be logged on to a computer.

You can take a practice test so that you can practise answering questions with the mouse and moving from one question to another. This practice test does not affect your final result in the real test.

When you are ready, the supervisor will tell you when you can begin your test and how long you have to complete it.

You will **not** be allowed to look at books or any notes you have made, and you will **not** be able to use any electronic device, such as a mobile phone, bluetooth headphones or palm pilot. If you are caught cheating, your test will be stopped immediately.

After the test

What happens if I pass the test?

If you pass the test, the test supervisor will give you a Pass Notification Letter that you must sign. The letter contains details of your test date, supervisor, centre location and a unique ID number.

You will need the Pass Notification Letter when you apply for citizenship or permanent residence, so it is very important to keep it safe.

When you have completed your application for citizenship or permanent residence, you need to attach your Pass Notification Letter and send both documents to the Home Office. The Home Office will keep the information it gets from test centres for a reasonable period of time. However, you should send in your application as soon as possible after taking the test.

What happens if I fail the test?

Your test supervisor will tell you if you have failed the test and will give you a Results Notification Letter. In this case you will need to take the test again. You will need to book and pay for another appointment and you will have to wait for at least seven days before you can retake the test.

You can take the test as many times as you need to. You cannot make an application for naturalisation as a British citizen or for indefinite leave to remain until you have passed the test.

If you feel you did not pass the test because of your level of English, you may want to think about going to combined English language (ESOL) and citizenship classes at your local further education college or adult education centre. If you do a course and get a certificate, you may not have to take the test again. English language requirements for settlement or citizenship may change and you should always check the up-to-date position on the UK Border Agency website.

Citizenship ceremony

If your application for citizenship is successful, the Home Office will send you a letter confirming this and inviting you to attend a ceremony. Your ceremony will usually be close to where you live. If you want your ceremony to be somewhere else in the UK, you need to make this clear when you make your application for naturalisation.

When you receive your invitation to a ceremony, you have 90 days to attend one. Your invitation will include contact details for the local authority or council that will organise your ceremony. The ceremony usually takes place at a register office or town hall, but it may take place in another public or community building.

You will usually be able to take two guests with you to the ceremony. Attendance at the ceremony is by invitation only.

It is also possible to arrange a private ceremony. You should discuss this with your local authority. You may have to pay an extra fee to arrange a private ceremony.

When you attend your ceremony, you must make an oath of allegiance (or you can make an affirmation if you prefer not to swear by God) and a pledge. These are the promises you make when you become a British citizen. The words of the oath, affirmation and pledge are all given below.

Oath of allegiance

I [name] swear by Almighty God that on becoming a British citizen, I will be faithful and bear true allegiance to Her Majesty Queen Elizabeth the Second, her Heirs and Successors, according to law.

Affirmation of allegiance

I [name] do solemnly, sincerely and truly declare and affirm that on becoming a British citizen, I will be faithful and bear true allegiance to Her Majesty Queen Elizabeth the Second, her Heirs and Successors, according to law.

Pledge

I will give my loyalty to the United Kingdom and respect its rights and freedoms. I will uphold its democratic values. I will observe its laws faithfully and fulfil my duties and obligations as a British citizen.

Ceremonies in Wales

If you are attending a ceremony in Wales you may, if you wish, make the oath or affirmation, and the pledge, in Welsh. The Welsh version of the oath, affirmation and pledge are below.

Llw teyrngarwch

Yr wyf i [enw], yn tyngu i Dduw Hollalluog y byddaf i, ar ôl dod yn ddinesydd Prydeinig, yn ffyddlon ac yn wir deyrngar i'w Mawrhydi y Frenhines Elisabeth yr Ail, ei Hetifeddion a'i Holynwyr, yn unol âr gyfraith.

Cadarnhau teyrngarwch

Yr wyf i [enw], yn datgan ac yn cadarnhau yn ddifrifol, yn ddiffuant ac yn gywir y byddaf i, ar ôl dod yn ddinesydd Prydeinig, yn ffyddlon ac yn wir deyrngar i'w Mawrhydi y Frenhines Elisabeth yr Ail, ei Hetifeddion a'i Holynwyr, yn unol âr gyfraith.

Adduned

Rhoddaf fy nheyrngarwch i'r Deyrnas Unedig ac fe barchaf ei hawliau a'i rhyddidau. Arddelaf ei gwerthoedd democrataidd. Glynaf yn ffyddlon wrth ei chyfreithiau a chyflawnaf fy nyletswyddau a'm rhwymedigaethau fel dinesydd Prydeinig.

Attending the ceremony

When you arrive at the ceremony, the staff will check your identity and confirm that the personal details on your certificate are correct.

During the ceremony, speeches will be made, often by important local or national people. These may include welcoming the new citizens on behalf of the local area and encouraging them to play an active role within their communities.

You will be presented with your certificate of British citizenship and a welcome pack. Sometimes new citizens receive a small gift from the council. All new citizens are invited to stand while the National Anthem is played.

Some local authorities arrange for photographs or videos of the event to be taken. You will be able to buy these if you would like to.

The values and
principles of the UK

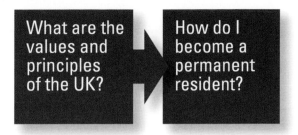

Britain is a diverse and dynamic nation which welcomes those who want to make a positive contribution to society.

By applying for citizenship, you agree to respect the laws, values and traditions of the UK.

Life in the United Kingdom: A Guide for New Residents and this accompanying study guide are designed to help you prepare for the test and integrate into society.

The values and principles of the UK

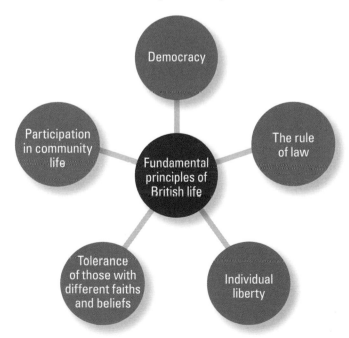

The values and principles of the UK are based on history and traditions. They are protected by law, customs and expectations. Extremism or intolerance is not acceptable in British society.

As a permanent resident or citizen of the UK you should:

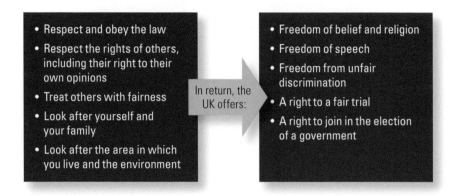

In return, the UK offers:

- Respect and obey the law
- Respect the rights of others, including their right to their own opinions
- Treat others with fairness
- Look after yourself and your family
- Look after the area in which you live and the environment

- Freedom of belief and religion
- Freedom of speech
- Freedom from unfair discrimination
- A right to a fair trial
- A right to join in the election of a government

Find out ...

✓ What pledge do you have to make to become a British citizen?

✓ How does passing the Life in the UK test help you as a citizen?

Becoming a permanent resident

To become a citizen or permanent resident you must:

- speak and read English
- pass a test to show you have a good understanding of life in the UK.

Once you have completed both of these tasks you can submit your application with the appropriate fee.

Find out ...

✓ About the tests you need to take and the documents you must provide as evidence of your language skills.

✓ How to take the Life in the UK test.

For further information

The following websites offer you more information about how to become a citizen:

The UK Border Agency (www.ukba.homeoffice.gov.uk) for more information about the application process and the forms you will need to complete.

The Life in the UK test website (www.lifeintheuktest.gov.uk) for more information about the test and how to book a place to take one.

Gov.uk (www.gov.uk) for information about ESOL courses and how to find one in your area.

Practice questions

Question 1   Which is a fundamental principle of British life?

☐ **A**   Actively supporting your local football team

☐ **B**   Participation in community life

☐ **C**   Ignoring your neighbours

☐ **D**   Eating fish on a Friday

Question 2   Which TWO things do you need to apply for UK citizenship or permanent residency?

☐ **A**   A knowledge of maths and science

☐ **B**   An understanding of life in the UK

☐ **C**   To speak and read English

☐ **D**   Access to a computer

Question 3   Is the statement below ☐ TRUE or ☐ FALSE?

All citizens and permanent residents of the UK can choose which laws they follow.

Question 4   Which of the following statements is correct?

☐ **A**   There is no place in British society for extremism or intolerance.

☐ **B**   Britain encourages people to have extreme views and to act upon them.

Question 5   Is the statement below ☐ TRUE or ☐ FALSE?

In the UK you are expected to treat others with fairness.

Question 6   What is a responsibility that you will have as a citizen or permanent resident of the UK?

☐ **A** Using your car as much as possible

☐ **B** Visiting your local pub regularly

☐ **C** Keeping an allotment

☐ **D** Looking after the environment

Answers and pointers to questions

Question	Answer	Explanation	Page reference in *Life in the United Kingdom: A Guide for New Residents*
1	B	Participation in community life is a fundamental principle of British life. British society is founded on fundamental values and principles which all those living in the UK should respect and support.	Pages 7–8
2	B and C	To apply to become a UK citizen or permanent resident, you must be able to speak and read English and have a good understanding of life in the UK.	Pages 8–9
3	FALSE	There are responsibilities and freedoms which are shared by all those living in the UK. These include respecting and obeying the law.	Page 8
4	A	There is no place for extremism or intolerance. British society is founded on fundamental values and principles which all those living in the UK respect and support.	Page 7
5	TRUE	There are responsibilities and freedoms which are shared by all those living in the UK. These include treating others with fairness.	Page 8
6	D	There are responsibilities and freedoms which are shared by all those living in the UK. These include looking after the environment, and the area in which you live.	Page 8

What is the UK?

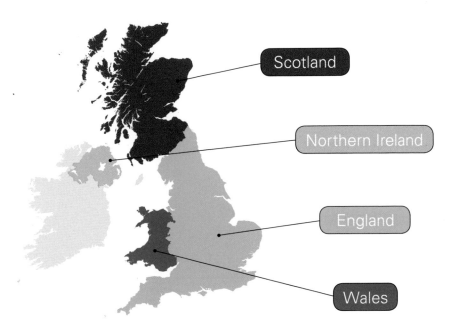

The United Kingdom is made up of England, Scotland, Wales and Northern Ireland.

The term 'Great Britain' does not include Northern Ireland.

People may refer to their nationality as British, English, Scottish, Welsh or Irish, but they all have British citizenship.

Find out ...

✓ What are the Crown dependencies and British overseas territories?

Practice questions

Question 1   Is the statement below ☐ TRUE or ☐ FALSE?

The Republic of Ireland is part of the UK.

Question 2   Which TWO of the following are part of the UK?

☐ **A**   Channel Islands

☐ **B**   Wales

☐ **C**   St Helena

☐ **D**   Scotland

Question 3   Which of the following is a British overseas territory?

☐ **A**   Solomon Islands

☐ **B**   Australia

☐ **C**   Falkland Islands

☐ **D**   Malta

Question 4   Is the statement below ☐ TRUE or ☐ FALSE?

The Isle of Man is a Crown dependency.

Question 5   Where is the UK Parliament based?

☐ **A**   Holyrood

☐ **B**   Senedd

☐ **C**   Stormont

☐ **D**   Westminster

Question 6   Which of the following statements is correct?

☐ **A** The official name of the UK is the United Kingdom of Great Britain and Northern Ireland.

☐ **B** The official name of the UK is Great Britain.

Answers and pointers to questions

Question	Answer	Explanation	Page reference in *Life in the United Kingdom: A Guide for New Residents*
1	FALSE	England, Scotland, Wales and Northern Ireland make up the UK.	Page 13
2	B and D	England, Scotland, Wales and Northern Ireland make up the UK.	Page 13
3	C	There are several British overseas territories in other parts of the world, such as the Falkland Islands.	Page 13
4	TRUE	The Isle of Man is a Crown dependency. It is closely linked with the UK but not part of it.	Page 13
5	D	The UK is governed by the parliament sitting in Westminster.	Page 13
6	A	The official name of the UK is the United Kingdom of Great Britain and Northern Ireland.	Page 13

A long and
illustrious history

Early Britain

The Stone Age

Britain was still connected to the continent of Europe until about 10,000 years ago. People were hunters-gatherers and followed the herds of horses and deer which provided their food and clothing.

The first farmers arrived in Britain 6,000 years ago. They built houses, tombs and monuments such as Stonehenge in Wiltshire. Skara Brae on Orkney, off the north coast of Scotland, is the best preserved prehistoric village in northern Europe.

The Bronze Age

About 4,000 years ago, people learned to make bronze. They made many beautiful objects in bronze and gold, including tools, ornaments and weapons. They lived in roundhouses and started to gather together in villages.

The Iron Age

People learned how to make weapons and tools out of iron. Villages grew larger and hill forts such as Maiden Castle, in Dorset, were built for defence. People at this time spoke a type of Celtic language that is related to Welsh and Gaelic. They made the first coins in Britain as the economy developed.

Find out ...

✓ Where did the first farmers come from?

✓ How has Skara Brae helped archaeologists?

✓ Where did people bury their dead in the Bronze Age?

✓ What occupations did people have in the Iron Age?

EARLY BRITAIN
- Stone, Bronze and Iron Ages
- The Romans
- The Anglo-Saxons
- The Vikings
- The Norman Conquest

THE MIDDLE AGES
- A time of war
- The Black Death
- Legal and political changes
- A distinct identity
- The Wars of the Roses

TUDORS AND STUARTS
- Religious conflicts
- Queen Elizabeth I
- The Reformation in Scotland and Mary, Queen of Scots
- Exploration, poetry and drama
- James VI and I
- Ireland
- The rise of Parliament
- The beginning of the English Civil War
- Oliver Cromwell and the English republic
- The Restoration
- A Catholic king
- The Glorious Revolution

The Romans

The Romans invaded Britain in AD 43 and remained for 400 years. Boudicca, the queen of the Iceni, in what is now eastern England, fought against the Romans.

A statue of Boudicca stands on Westminster Bridge in London

A GLOBAL POWER
- Constitutional monarchy and the Prime Minister
- A free press
- A growing population
- The rebellion of the clans
- The Enlightenment
- The Industrial Revolution
- The slave trade
- The American War of Independence
- War with France
- The Union Flag
- The Victorian Age
- Migration and the British Empire
- Trade and industry
- The Crimean War
- Ireland in the 19th century
- The right to vote
- The future of the Empire

THE 20th CENTURY
- The First World War
- The partition of Ireland
- The inter-war period
- The Second World War

BRITAIN SINCE 1945
- The welfare state
- Migration in post-war Britain
- Social and technological change in the 1960s
- Some great British inventions of the 20th century
- Problems in the economy in the 1970s
- Northern Ireland
- Europe and the Common Market
- Conservative government from 1979 to 1997
- Labour government from 1997 to 2010
- Conflicts in Afghanistan and Iraq
- Coalition government 2010 onwards

The Romans never succeeded in conquering all of Scotland, and Hadrian's Wall was built to keep out the Picts (ancestors of the Scottish people).

The Romans built roads and public buildings, created a structure of law, and introduced new plants and animals. During the 3rd and 4th centuries AD the first Christian communities began to appear in Britain.

Find out …

✓ How long were the Romans in Britain?

✓ Why is Hadrian's Wall attractive to tourists?

✓ Where will you find a statue of Boudicca?

The Anglo-Saxons

When the Roman army left in AD 410, Britain was invaded by the Jutes, Angles and Saxons. The languages they spoke are the basis of modern-day English. By about AD 600, Anglo-Saxon kingdoms were established in Britain.

The Anglo-Saxons were not Christians but the country was gradually converted when missionaries came to Britain to preach about Christianity. St Augustine led missionaries from Rome and became the first Archbishop of Canterbury.

Find out …

✓ Why did the Romans leave Britain?

✓ Where and how was one of the Anglo-Saxon kings buried?

✓ Who spread Christianity to the north and south of Britain?

The Vikings

The Vikings, from Denmark and Norway, first visited Britain in AD 789 to raid coastal towns and take away goods and slaves. They began to settle and form their own communities in the east of England and Scotland, but were defeated in England by King Alfred the Great. Many of the Vikings decided to live in Britain. The Viking settlers mixed with local communities and some converted to Christianity.

In the north, Viking attacks encouraged the people to unite under one king, Kenneth MacAlpin. The term Scotland began to be used to describe that country.

Find out …

✓ What was the Danelaw?

✓ Who was the first Danish king to rule England?

The Norman Conquest

In 1066, William, Duke of Normandy, defeated Harold, the Saxon king of England, at the Battle of Hastings. Harold was killed in the battle. William became king of England and is known as William the Conqueror. The Bayeux Tapestry commemorates the battle and can still be seen in France today.

The Norman Conquest was the last successful foreign invasion of England.

It led to many changes in government and social structures in England. The English language today shows the influence of Norman French.

Find out …

✓ What impact did the Norman Conquest have on Wales and Scotland?

✓ What is the Domesday Book and how was its content collected?

The Middle Ages

A time of war

The Middle Ages followed the Norman Conquest. It was a time of almost constant war.

- Wales was annexed to the English crown.
- The Scots remained independent.
- Ireland gradually came under the influence of England.

There were also wars abroad. Knights took part in the Crusades, in which European Christians fought to control the Holy Land.

English kings also fought the Hundred Years War with France. The English left France in the 1450s. The armies were provided by landowners who had been given land by the king. This was known as feudalism. Some peasants had their own land but most were serfs. They had a small area of their lord's land where they could grow food. In return, they had to work for their lord and could not move away. The same system developed in southern Scotland. In the north of Scotland and Ireland, land was owned by members of the 'clans'.

The Black Death

In 1348, one-third of the population of England, and a similar proportion in Scotland and Wales, died from a form of plague, known as the Black Death.

There was a shortage of people to work on the land and the peasants began to demand higher wages. New social classes appeared and people left the countryside to live in the towns. This all led to the development of a strong middle class.

In Ireland, the Black Death killed many in the Pale (English-controlled areas).

Find out ...

✓ About the wars between England and Wales, Scotland and Ireland.

✓ Name a famous battle in the Hundred Years War.

✓ What was the feudal system and how was it introduced?

✓ How did the Black Death lead to the development of a strong middle class?

Legal and political changes

The origins of the UK Parliament are in the Middle Ages.

In 1215 King John was forced by his noblemen to agree to the Magna Carta. In future the king would have to consult the noblemen if he wanted to collect taxes or change laws. This developed into Parliament.

As it grew, Parliament in England was divided into two parts:

- the House of Lords for the nobility, great landowners and bishops
- the House of Commons for knights, who were usually smaller landowners, and wealthy people from towns and cities. The electorate was very small.

Parliament also developed in Scotland. It had three Houses, called Estates: the lords, the commons and the clergy.

In 1215 King John was forced by his noblemen to agree to the Magna Carta

Judges became independent of government and 'common law' developed in England. In Scotland the legal system developed slightly differently.

Find out ...

✓ What does Magna Carta mean?

✓ What were its implications for the monarch's power?

✓ How did the legal system develop in Scotland?

A distinct identity

A national culture and identity started to develop in the Middle Ages. In England, Norman French (spoken by the king and his court) and Anglo-Saxon (spoken by the peasants) merged into one English language. English had become the preferred language of the royal court and Parliament by 1400.

Geoffrey Chaucer wrote a series of poems in English about a group of people going to Canterbury on a pilgrimage. It was one of the earliest books to be printed by William Caxton, the first person in England to print books using a printing press.

In Scotland many people continued to speak Gaelic, and the Scots language also developed.

You will find many buildings which date from the Middle Ages. There are many castles, some of which are in ruins, in Britain and Ireland. Some are still in use. Beautiful cathedrals are also found across the country. Many have stained-glass windows which tell Bible stories.

England became an important trading nation. Wool was exported and people came to trade and work.

Find out ...

✓ Give some examples of English words which come from Norman French and Anglo-Saxon.

✓ What language was used for official documents by 1400?

✓ What were *The Canterbury Tales* about?

✓ Who was William Caxton?

✓ Give an example of a poem written in the Scots language.

✓ Give some examples of castles and cathedrals in Britain.

✓ What skills did people bring to England from other countries?

The Wars of the Roses

The Wars of the Roses were fought in 1455. Supporters of the House of York, whose symbol was a white rose, and the House of Lancaster, whose symbol was a red rose, battled to decide who would be king of England.

The House of Lancaster beat the House of York at the Battle of Bosworth Field and Henry Tudor became King Henry VII.

Find out ...

✓ When did the Battle of Bosworth Field take place and what was the outcome?

✓ How were the Houses of York and Lancaster united?

✓ Explain how the Tudor rose was formed.

The Tudors and Stuarts

Religious conflicts

To keep England peaceful and maintain his power, Henry VII strengthened the central administration of England and reduced the power of the nobles. He also built up the monarchy's financial reserves. His son, Henry VIII, continued the policy of centralising power.

Henry VIII was most famous for breaking away from the Church of Rome and marrying six times.

Henry VII holding a red rose, the symbol of the House of Lancaster

The Pope refused to allow Henry to divorce his first wife, so Henry set up the Church of England. The king, not the Pope, would have the power to appoint bishops and order how people should worship.

At the same time the Reformation was happening across Europe.

In Ireland the English attempted to impose Protestantism and the English system of laws about the inheritance of land. This led to rebellion from the Irish chieftains.

In this period, Wales became united with England by the Act for the Government of Wales.

Henry VIII's son succeeded him. Edward VI was strongly Protestant and, during his reign, the Book of Common Prayer was written for use in the Church of England. Edward was only 15 when he died, after ruling for just over six years.

Mary, his half-sister, became queen. She was a devout Catholic and persecuted Protestants. Mary died after a short reign and the next monarch was her half-sister Elizabeth.

Find out ...

✓ What do you know about the wives of Henry VIII?

✓ What effect did the Reformation have in Europe?

✓ How was Wales represented after the Act for the Government of Wales?

✓ What was Queen Mary known as? Explain why.

✓ Who were Elizabeth I's parents?

Queen Elizabeth I

Queen Elizabeth I was a Protestant but avoided any serious religious conflict in England. Elizabeth became one of the most popular monarchs in English history, particularly after 1588, when the English defeated the Spanish Armada (a large fleet of ships), which had been sent by Spain to conquer England and restore Catholicism.

The Reformation in Scotland and Mary, Queen of Scots

Scotland had also been strongly influenced by Protestant ideas, and a Protestant Church of Scotland with an elected leadership was established.

The queen of Scotland, Mary Stuart (often now called 'Mary, Queen of Scots'), was a Catholic. She was only a week old when her father died and she became queen.

Find out ...

✓ How did Elizabeth I avoid religious conflict in England?

✓ How did the establishment of the Protestant Church of Scotland affect the country?

✓ What happened to Mary, Queen of Scots?

Exploration, poetry and drama

The Elizabethan period in England was a time of growing patriotism: a feeling of pride in being English. English explorers sought new trade routes and tried to expand British trade into the Spanish colonies in the Americas.

The Elizabethan period is also remembered for the richness of its poetry and drama, especially the plays and poems of William Shakespeare.

Shakespeare was born in Stratford-upon-Avon, England. He was a playwright and actor and wrote many poems and plays. His most famous plays include *A Midsummer Night's Dream*, *Hamlet*, *Macbeth* and *Romeo and Juliet*. His plays and poems are still performed and studied in Britain and other countries today. The Globe Theatre in London is a modern copy of the theatres in which his plays were first performed.

Find out …

✓ What did Francis Drake do?

✓ Where did English settlers first begin to colonise, during and after Elizabeth I's reign?

✓ What topics do Shakespeare's plays explore?

✓ Give five quotations from Shakespeare's plays.

James VI and I

Elizabeth I never married and had no children to inherit her throne. When she died in 1603 her cousin James VI of Scotland was her heir. He became King James I of England, Wales and Ireland but Scotland remained a separate country.

Ireland

During the reigns of Elizabeth I and James I, there were a number of rebellions, because many Irish people opposed rule from England. Land was taken from Catholic landholders and given to Protestant settlers from England and Scotland. These settlements were known as plantations. This had serious long-term consequences for the history of England, Scotland and Ireland.

Find out …

✓ What is the King James Bible?

✓ What role did Henry VII and Henry VIII have in Ireland?

The rise of Parliament

James I and his son Charles I were less successful than Elizabeth I in managing Parliament. They believed in the 'Divine Right of Kings': the idea that the king was directly appointed by God to rule. They did not accept the need to consult Parliament.

When Charles I became king of England, Wales, Ireland and Scotland, he tried to rule in line with this principle. For 11 years, he found ways to raise money without Parliament's approval.

The beginning of the English Civil War

Charles I tried to impose his version of the Prayer Book on the Presbyterian Church in Scotland. A Scottish army was formed and, in 1640, Charles had to recall Parliament to raise the funds for his own army. The Puritans in Parliament did not like the king's religious views and refused to give him the money.

A rebellion in Ireland led to Parliament demanding control of the army. Charles I objected because his power would have been lost. He entered the House of Commons to arrest the leaders, but they had been warned and were not there.

This led to the outbreak of civil war in 1642. The country was divided between people who supported the king (Cavaliers) and those who supported Parliament (Roundheads).

Find out ...

✓ Who were the Puritans?

✓ Why did they refuse to give the king money?

✓ Why was there a rebellion in Ireland?

Oliver Cromwell and the English republic

The king's army lost the war and Charles I was executed in 1649.

England became a republic, called the Commonwealth. The army was in control. Oliver Cromwell, one of its generals, was sent to Ireland to establish the authority of the English Parliament.

As the Scots had not agreed to the execution of Charles I, they declared his son Charles II to be king. He led a Scottish army into England but was defeated by Cromwell. Parliament now controlled Scotland as well as England and Wales.

Cromwell became Lord Protector and ruled until his death in 1658. His son, Richard, became Lord Protector on his death but could not control the army or the government. People began to talk about the need for a king.

Find out ...

✓ The names of some of the battles fought during the Civil War.

✓ How did Cromwell deal with the Irish rebellion?

✓ What happened to Charles II when he escaped after the Battle of Worcester?

The Restoration

The restoration of the monarchy happened in 1660, when Parliament invited Charles II to come back from exile and be crowned king

Charles II was crowned king of England, Wales, Scotland and Ireland in 1660. He understood that he would have to work with Parliament. Generally, Parliament supported his policies. The Church of England became the established church again.

The Habeas Corpus Act became law in 1679. This was a very important piece of legislation which remains relevant today. Habeas Corpus is Latin for 'you must present the person in court'. The Act guaranteed that no one could be held prisoner unlawfully. Every prisoner has a right to a court hearing.

Find out …

✓ When the Church of England again became the official church, what did this mean for Catholics and Puritans?

✓ What great events took place during the reign of Charles II?

✓ What is the Royal Society and when was it founded?

✓ Who was Isaac Newton and what did he do?

A Catholic king

Charles II died in 1685 and his brother, James, a Roman Catholic, became King James II in England, Wales and Ireland and King James VII of Scotland. People in England worried that James wanted to make England a Catholic country. His two daughters were both Protestant, and it had seemed likely that one would become queen. But when James's wife had a son, people feared that the next monarch would be Catholic after all.

Find out …

✓ Why did James II become king?

✓ What did James II do to some of the Church of England bishops?

The Glorious Revolution

James II's daughter, Mary, was married to William of Orange, the Protestant ruler of the Netherlands. In 1688, on the invitation of important Protestants, William arrived in England. James fled to France and William took over the throne jointly with Mary, becoming William III in England, Wales and Ireland, and William II of Scotland. This was later called the 'Glorious Revolution' because there was no fighting and it guaranteed the power of Parliament.

The French helped James II to invade Ireland, but William re-conquered it and James fled back to France. Many restrictions were placed on the Roman Catholic Church in Ireland and Irish Catholics were banned from government.

Some people in Scotland supported James but they were defeated. All Scottish clans had to accept William as king and take an oath. When the MacDonalds of Glencoe were late taking the oath, they were all killed. This massacre meant some Scots distrusted the new government.

Find out ...

✓ What was the name of battle in Ireland in which William defeated James II, and when did it take place?

✓ Who were the Jacobites?

A global power

Constitutional monarchy and the Prime Minister

A Declaration of Rights was read at the coronation of William and Mary. It confirmed the king could not raise taxes or administer justice without Parliament. The monarch needed to have advisers, or ministers, who had the support of the House of Commons and the House of

Lords. The Whigs and the Tories were the two main groups in Parliament. (The modern Conservative Party is still sometimes referred to as 'the Tories'.) This was the beginning of party politics.

The balance of power between monarch and Parliament had permanently changed. The Bill of Rights in 1689 confirmed these changes. The king had become a 'constitutional monarch'.

Very few people had the vote and there were many 'rotten' boroughs.

The Kingdom of Great Britain was created when the Act of Union, known as the Treaty of Union in Scotland, was agreed in 1707. This was done to ensure there would be continuity when Queen Anne died, as she had no direct heirs. Although Scotland was no longer an independent country, it kept its own legal and education systems and the Presbyterian Church.

Parliament chose George I, a German, to be king in 1714. He did not speak good English and needed to rely on his ministers. The most important minister became known as the Prime Minister.

Find out ...

✓ What did the Declaration of Rights state?

✓ Who were the Whigs and the Tories?

✓ How did the Bill of Rights in 1689 change the role of the monarch and Parliament?

✓ What is a constitutional monarch?

✓ Who didn't have the vote at this time?

✓ What is a rotten borough?

✓ Why did Parliament choose George I to be king?

✓ Who was the first Prime Minister and how long did he hold this position?

A free press

From 1695, newspapers were allowed to operate without a government licence. Increasing numbers of newspapers began to be published. It was the beginning of a free press.

Find out …

✓ What is meant by 'a free press'?

A growing population

The new colonies in America and elsewhere were growing as people left Britain but others were coming to live here. Jews arrived and Huguenots came from France. Many were educated and skilled and worked as scientists, in banking, or in weaving or other crafts.

Find out …

✓ When did the Jews and Huguenots arrive?

✓ Why did the Huguenots leave France?

The rebellion of the clans

In 1745 there was attempt to put a Stuart king on the throne in place of George I's son, George II. Charles Edward Stuart was defeated by George II's army at the Battle of Culloden in 1746 and escaped back to Europe.

The clans lost a lot of their power after Culloden. Chieftains became landlords if they had the favour of the English king, and clansmen became tenants who had to pay for the land they used. A process began which became known as the 'Highland Clearances'.

Robert Burns was a Scottish poet who wrote in the Scots language, English with some Scottish words, and standard English.

> **Find out ...**
>
> ✓ What was Charles Edward Stuart known as?
>
> ✓ Who supported Charles Edward Stuart?
>
> ✓ What were the Highland Clearances?
>
> ✓ Who was Robert Burns, when did he live and what did he do?

The Enlightenment

The Enlightenment, which occurred in the 18th century, brought new ideas in politics, philosophy and science. A key principle was that people should be free to choose their own religious and political beliefs, and the state should not be able to challenge them. This principle is still an important element of British society.

> **Find out ...**
>
> ✓ Name two key thinkers and a scientist who worked during the Enlightenment.

The Industrial Revolution

The key facts of the Industrial Revolution are as follows:

- Until the 18th century the UK was mainly agricultural. Small-scale industry, such as cloth making, was often found in people's homes.
- The Industrial Revolution took place as the development of water power and then steam power led to the growth of factories. People left the countryside to work in the factories, so towns and cities grew.
- As the economy developed during the 19th century, canals and railways were built across the country.
- Richard Arkwright developed machinery to make the textile industry more efficient.

- The Bessemer process for the mass production of steel led to the development of the shipbuilding industry and the railways. Manufacturing jobs became the main source of employment in Britain.

- Canals were built to link the factories to towns and cities and to the ports, particularly in the new industrial areas in the middle and north of England.

- Working conditions were very poor. Adults and children were often forced to work long hours in dangerous situations.

At the time of the Industrial Revolution, Britain's colonies expanded in Australia, Canada and southern Africa. The East India Company gained control of large parts of India.

Britain traded all over the world and began to import more goods. Trading and settlements overseas brought Britain into conflict with France.

The colonies influenced life in Britain. Sake Dean Mahomet, for example, opened the first curry house in Britain. Mahomet and his wife also introduced 'shampooing', the Indian art of head massage, to Britain.

Large factories using steam power were built during the Industrial Revolution

Find out ...

✓ Why were canals and railways necessary?

✓ How did Richard Arkwright make the textile industry more efficient?

✓ What goods did the UK trade with the rest of the world?

✓ Why did trade bring conflict?

The slave trade

Slaves from West Africa were taken to America in horrible conditions on British ships. They worked on tobacco and sugar plantations and were very badly treated.

William Wilberforce, an evangelical Christian and a member of Parliament, succeeded in turning public opinion against the slave trade. In 1807, it became illegal to trade slaves in British ships or from British ports, and in 1833 the Emancipation Act abolished slavery throughout the British Empire.

Find out ...

✓ Which religious group opposed the slave trade?

✓ What was the role of the Royal Navy after slavery was banned?

✓ Where did workers come from to replace the slaves?

The American War of Independence

Many of the colonists in North America had left Britain for religious freedom. They saw Britain's desire to tax them as an attack on their freedom and said there should be 'no taxation without representation'. Parliament tried to compromise by repealing some of the taxes, but eventually fighting broke out between the colonists and the British forces. The colonists defeated the British army and Britain recognised their independence in 1783.

War with France

Napoleon, Emperor of France, was at war with Britain. Britain's navy fought the French and Spanish fleets, winning the Battle of Trafalgar in 1805. Admiral Nelson was in charge of the British fleet at Trafalgar and was killed in the battle. The British army also fought the French. In 1815, Napoleon was defeated by the Duke of Wellington at the Battle of Waterloo.

Find out ...

✓ Why did the American colonies fight the British army and what was the outcome?

✓ Where is Nelson commemorated and where can his ship be seen?

✓ What did Wellington do after fighting the French?

The Union Flag

The United Kingdom of Great Britain and Ireland was created when the Act of Union was passed in 1800. The Union Flag represented the new kingdom. It is often called the Union Jack and is made up of the crosses of England, Scotland and Ireland.

The Union Flag, also known as the Union Jack

The Welsh dragon does not appear on the Union Flag because the Principality of Wales was already united with England.

Find out ...

✓ Which of the crosses represents each country of the United Kingdom?

The Victorian Age

Queen Victoria became queen of the United Kingdom in 1837 when she was 18. She reigned for almost 64 years. This is known as the Victorian Age. Britain's power and influence abroad was increasing. The middle classes were increasingly significant and a number of reformers worked to improve conditions for the poor.

Migration and the British Empire

The British Empire grew to cover all of India, Australia and large parts of Africa. It had an estimated population of more than 400 million people. Between 1853 and 1913, 13 million people left the UK to settle overseas. People from the Empire, including India and Africa, also came to Britain to live, work and study.

Between 1870 and 1914, around 120,000 Russian and Polish Jews came to Britain. They settled predominantly in London's East End, Manchester and Leeds.

Find out ...

✓ Why did Russian and Polish Jews come to the UK?

Trade and industry

The government began to promote free trade, abolishing a number of taxes on imported goods. One example was the repeal of the Corn Laws in 1846.

Working conditions in factories gradually improved, and better housing was built for workers.

Improvements in transport links allowed goods and people to move more easily around the country. George and Robert Stephenson and Isambard Kingdom Brunel contributed to these developments.

In the 19th century the UK produced more than half of the world's iron, coal and cotton cloth. It was a centre for financial services, including insurance and banking. In 1851, the Great Exhibition opened in Hyde Park in the Crystal Palace, a huge building made of steel and glass.

Find out ...

✓ Why did the government repeal the Corn Laws?

✓ How did working conditions for women and children improve?

✓ How did George and Robert Stephenson and Isambard Kingdom Brunel improve transport in the UK and the Empire?

✓ What was on show at the Great Exhibition?

The Crimean War

In the Crimean War Britain fought with Turkey and France against Russia. It was the first war to be covered extensively by the media. Many soldiers died because of illnesses in the hospitals. Florence Nightingale improved the conditions in hospitals and reduced mortality rates.

During this war, Queen Victoria introduced the Victoria Cross, which honours acts of valour by soldiers.

Find out ...

✓ How did Florence Nightingale influence British nursing?

Ireland in the 19th century

Many people in Ireland lived in poor conditions and depended on growing potatoes. In the middle of the 19th century, the crop failed and a million people died from disease and starvation. Many people emigrated to escape the famine.

The Irish Nationalist movement had grown strongly through the 19th century. The Fenians favoured complete independence. Charles Stuart Parnell wanted 'Home Rule', in which Ireland would remain in the UK but have its own parliament.

Find out ...

✓ Where did Irish emigrants go in the 19th century?

✓ Which cities in Britain had large Irish populations?

The right to vote

The Reform Act of 1832 increased the number of people with the right to vote, but members of the working class were still excluded.

The Chartists wanted to extend the vote further. In 1867 there was another Reform Act, which extended the vote but still excluded the majority of men and all women.

More voters meant that politicians needed to persuade people to vote for them. The political parties began to create organisations to reach out to ordinary voters.

In common with the rest of Europe, women had fewer rights than men. When a woman got married, all her property belonged to her husband. Acts of Parliament in 1870 and 1882 changed this.

Emmeline Pankhurst was one of the leading campaigners of the women's suffrage movement

The women's suffrage movement campaigned for the right to vote. Campaigners became known as 'suffragettes'. Emmeline Pankhurst was one of the leading campaigners.

In 1928 women were given the right to vote at the age of 21, the same as men.

Find out ...

✓ How did the Reform Act of 1832 change voting in the UK?

✓ How did Emmeline Pankhurst contribute to the suffrage movement?

✓ How did the suffragettes campaign for the vote?

The future of the Empire

In the early 20th century, people began to ask questions about the future of the Empire. Some thought it should continue to grow because it brought wealth to the UK and benefited the world. Rudyard Kipling wrote books and poems reflecting the strengths of the Empire.

Others thought it was a drain on resources because of conflicts and countries' growing desire for independence. By the second half of the 20th century the transition from Empire to Commonwealth was orderly for the most part, as countries were granted their independence.

Find out …

✓ Where were conflicts taking place in the Empire?

✓ How did the Boer War affect people's views on the Empire?

✓ How did the change from Empire to Commonwealth take place?

✓ Who was Rudyard Kipling and what did he write?

The 20th century

Financial help for the unemployed

Salaries for MPs so more people could take part in public life

Old-age pensions

Local government became more democratic

In the period before the First World War, life was improving for many people

Free school meals

Support for mothers and children after divorce or separation

Town planning rules prevented the development of slums

Laws on safety in the workplace

The First World War

The First World War broke out after the assassination of Archduke Franz Ferdinand of Austria, but many other factors were involved.

The conflict was centred in Europe, yet it was a global war involving nations from around the world. Millions of people were killed or wounded, with more than 2 million British casualties. One battle, the British attack on the Somme in July 1916, resulted in about 60,000 British casualties on the first day alone.

The First World War ended at 11.00 am on 11 November 1918 with victory for Britain and its allies.

Find out …

✓ Why did the First World War happen?

✓ Which countries were involved in the First World War?

The British Cemetery on the battlefields of the Somme, France

The partition of Ireland

In 1913, the British government promised 'Home Rule' for Ireland. The Protestants in the north of Ireland opposed it. At the outbreak of the First World War the British government postponed any changes in Ireland, but the Irish Nationalists were not willing to wait.

This resulted in the Easter Rising against the British. The leaders of the uprising were executed and a guerrilla war broke out against the British army and the police. In 1921 a peace treaty was signed and in 1922 Ireland became two countries. Northern Ireland, which was mainly Protestant, remained part of the UK. The rest of Ireland became the Irish Free State. It had its own government and became a republic in 1949.

People in both parts of Ireland disagreed with the split. This eventually led to a terror campaign, often called 'the Troubles'.

Find out ...

✓ Why did the Easter Rising take place?

✓ What were 'the Troubles'?

The inter-war period

In the 1920s, many people's living conditions got better. There were improvements in public housing and new homes were built in many towns and cities. In 1929, the 'Great Depression' affected the world, and some parts of the UK suffered mass unemployment. The effects of the depression of the 1930s were felt differently in different parts of the UK.

The inter-war period was also a time of cultural change:

- Writers such as Graham Greene and Evelyn Waugh became prominent.
- John Maynard Keynes published influential new theories of economics.

- The BBC started radio broadcasts in 1922 and began the world's first regular television service in 1936.

Find out ...

✓ How did people's lives improve in the 1920s?

✓ How did different parts of the country suffer in the Great Depression?

✓ How did industry develop in this period?

The Second World War

Adolf Hitler came to power in Germany in 1933. He wanted to spread German power and felt that the conditions imposed on Germany after the First World War were unfair. The British government tried to avoid another war but, when Hitler invaded Poland in 1939, Britain and France declared war in order to stop him.

By 1940, Germany had occupied Austria, invaded Czechoslovakia and Poland, and taken control of Belgium and the Netherlands. German troops then advanced through France. At this time of national crisis, Winston Churchill became Prime Minister and Britain's war leader.

British and French soldiers were evacuated from Dunkirk in France. Many lives and a lot of equipment were lost, but the evacuation was a success and Britain was able to continue fighting the Germans. The evacuation gave rise to the phrase 'the Dunkirk spirit'.

Hitler wanted to invade Britain but needed to control the air first. The Germans waged an air campaign against Britain but were finally defeated in 'the Battle of Britain' in the summer of 1940.

Despite this crucial victory, the German air force was able to continue bombing London and other British cities. This was called the Blitz. The phrase 'the Blitz spirit' is still used today to describe Britons pulling together in the face of adversity.

Parts of Britain were bombed by German air campaigns during the Second Wold War, in what is known as the Blitz

While defending Britain, British forces were fighting the Axis powers (Germany, Italy and Japan) on many other fronts. The Japanese defeated the British in Singapore and then occupied Burma, threatening India. In December 1941, the United States entered the war when the Japanese bombed its naval base at Pearl Harbour.

That same year, Hitler attempted to invade the Soviet Union. Germany was repelled and the resulting damage proved to be a turning point in the war.

The Allies won significant victories in North Africa and Italy. With the support of the Americans, the Allies could attack Hitler's forces in Western Europe. On 6 June 1944 ('D-Day'), allied forces fought the German troops on the beaches of Normandy. They then drove them back through France and into Germany. The Allies finally defeated Germany in the summer of 1945.

The war against Japan ended in August 1945 when the United States dropped atom bombs on the Japanese cities of Hiroshima and Nagasaki. The war was finally over.

Find out ...

✓ How did Hitler set about building Germany's power?

✓ Which countries were involved in the Second World War?

✓ Who was Winston Churchill and what did he do?

✓ How were troops evacuated from Dunkirk?

✓ What planes did the British use in the Battle of Britain?

✓ Name some of the cities damaged in the Blitz.

✓ What role did the UK have in the development of the atom bomb?

Alexander Fleming (1881–1955)

Alexander Fleming was born in Scotland, then moved to London, where he qualified as a doctor. He won the Nobel Prize in Medicine in 1945 for his discovery of penicillin, which is still used to treat bacterial infections today.

Find out ...

✓ Which two scientists turned penicillin into a usable drug?

Britain since 1945

The welfare state

Despite winning the war, the UK was exhausted economically and people wanted change. In 1945 the British people elected a Labour government. The new Prime Minister was Clement Attlee, who promised to introduce the welfare state outlined in the Beveridge Report.

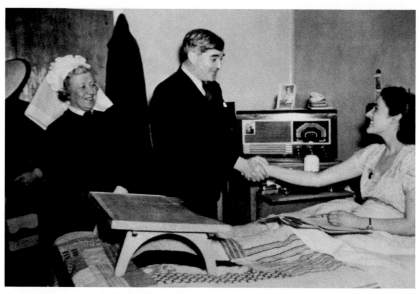

Aneurin Bevan set up the National Health Service

In 1948, Aneurin (Nye) Bevan, the Minister for Health, set up the National Health Service (NHS), which gave health care for all, free at the point of use.

A system of benefits was introduced to provide 'social security', to protect people from the 'cradle to the grave'.

The government nationalised the railways, coal mines and gas, water and electricity supplies.

The year 1947 brought the start of changes in the Empire. Nine countries became independent, including India, Pakistan and Ceylon (now Sri Lanka). Over the next 20 years many other countries became independent.

The UK developed its own atomic bomb and joined the North Atlantic Treaty Organization (NATO).

The 1950s were a period of economic recovery after the war and increasing prosperity for working people. A Conservative government was in power from 1951 to 1964. Harold Macmillan was Prime Minister for some of this period.

Find out ...

✓ What do you know about the life and work of:

- Clement Attlee (1883–1967)?
- William Beveridge (1879–1963)?
- R A Butler (1902–82)?

✓ What is NATO?

✓ Who was Harold Macmillan and what was he famous for?

Dylan Thomas (1914–53)

Dylan Thomas was a Welsh poet and writer. He often performed his work in public, including for the BBC. He died in New York, aged 39. There are memorials to him in his birthplace, Swansea.

Find out ...

✓ What famous works did Dylan Thomas write?

✓ What memorials are there of Dylan Thomas?

Migration in post-war Britain

After the Second World War there were labour shortages, and workers from Ireland, other parts of Europe and the West Indies were invited to come and work in the UK.

In the late 1960s immigration fell because of new laws restricting immigration to Britain. Despite this, 28,000 people of Indian origin, who had been expelled from Uganda, came to Britain in the early 1970s.

Social and technological change in the 1960s

The decade of the 1960s was called 'the Swinging Sixties' because of the growth in British fashion, cinema and popular music. People were better off and bought cars and other consumer goods.

Social laws were changing in many fields, such as:

- divorce
- abortion
- equal pay for women
- gender discrimination.

The 1960s was also a time of technological progress. Britain and France developed Concorde, the world's only supersonic commercial airliner. High-rise buildings of concrete and steel became common as architecture developed.

Some great British inventions of the 20th century

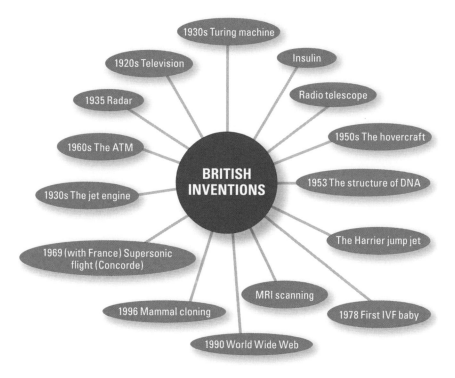

Find out …

✓ How were people attracted to come to Britain to work?

✓ Name two well-known pop groups of the 1960s.

✓ Did divorce and abortion laws change throughout the UK?

✓ What criteria did people need to meet to come to live in Britain in the late 1960s?

✓ What else do you know about the great British inventions of the 20th century?

Problems in the economy in the 1970s

In the late 1970s, the post-war economic boom came to an end. As a result:

● the price of goods and raw materials rose sharply

● the exchange rate became unstable

● there were problems with the 'balance of payments'

● strikes took place in many industries

● some people thought the unions were too powerful.

Find out …

✓ Why was there a problem with the 'balance of payments' in the 1970s?

✓ Why did people think that the trade unions were too powerful in the 1970s?

Northern Ireland

In the 1970s there was serious unrest in Northern Ireland. The Northern Ireland Parliament was suspended in 1972 and the country was directly ruled by the UK government.

Europe and the Common Market

In 1957 West Germany, France, Belgium, Italy, Luxembourg and the Netherlands formed the European Economic Community (EEC). The UK did not join the EEC until 1973. The UK is a full member of the European Union, but does not use the Euro as currency.

Conservative government from 1979 to 1997

Margaret Thatcher, Britain's first woman Prime Minister, led the Conservative government from 1979 to 1990.

The government introduced the following policies:

- privatisation of nationalised industries
- legal controls on trade union powers.

Deregulation of the City of London led to its growth as an international centre for investments, insurance and other financial services.

Traditional industries, such as shipbuilding and coal mining, declined. In 1982, Argentina invaded the Falkland Islands and the British Navy regained control.

John Major was Prime Minister after Margaret Thatcher, and helped establish the Northern Ireland peace process.

Find out ...

✓ What do you know about the life and work of Margaret Thatcher?

Roald Dahl (1916–90)

Roald Dahl is well known for his children's books such as *Charlie and the Chocolate Factory* and *George's Marvellous Medicine*. Several of his books have been made into films. He also wrote books for adults.

> **Find out ...**
>
> ✓ What do you know about the life of Roald Dahl?

Labour government from 1997 to 2010

In 1997 the Labour Party won the General Election. It was led by Tony Blair, who became Prime Minister. The Scottish Parliament and Welsh Assembly were established during the Blair government.

In 1998 the Good Friday Agreement, which brought peace to Northern Ireland, was signed. The Northern Ireland Assembly was elected in 1999 but suspended in 2002. It was reinstated in 2007. Most paramilitary groups in Northern Ireland are inactive.

Gordon Brown took over as Prime Minister in 2007.

> **Find out ...**
>
> ✓ What powers do the Scottish Parliament and Welsh Assembly have?

Conflicts in Afghanistan and Iraq

Throughout the 1990s, Britain played a leading role in coalition forces involved in the liberation of Kuwait, following the Iraqi invasion in 1990, and the conflict in the former Republic of Yugoslavia. Since 2000, British armed forces have been engaged in the global fight against international terrorism and against the proliferation of weapons of mass destruction, including operations in Afghanistan and Iraq. British combat troops left Iraq in 2009. The UK now operates in Afghanistan as part of the United Nations (UN) mandated 50-nation International Security Assistance Force (ISAF) coalition and at the invitation of the Afghan government. ISAF is working to ensure that Afghan territory can never again be used as a safe haven for international terrorism, where groups such as Al Qa'ida could plan attacks on the international community. As part of this, ISAF is building up the Afghan National

Security Forces and is helping to create a secure environment in which governance and development can be extended. International forces are gradually handing over responsibility for security to the Afghans, who will have full security responsibility in all provinces by the end of 2014.

Coalition government 2010 onwards

After the General Election in May 2010, no political party won an overall majority.

David Cameron became Prime Minister, leading a coalition government made up of the Conservatives and Liberal Democrats.

Practice questions

Question 1   Which TWO did the Reform Act of 1832 bring about?

☐ **A**   More people were given the right to vote.

☐ **B**   The first-ever Prime Minister was appointed.

☐ **C**   Women over 25 were given the right to vote.

☐ **D**   More parliamentary seats were given to towns and cities.

Question 2   Who did Britain fight against in the Crimean War?

☐ **A**   Russia

☐ **B**   Turkey

☐ **C**   France

☐ **D**   Japan

Question 3   In what year did women first get the vote?

☐ **A**   1882

☐ **B**   1918

☐ **C**   1939

☐ **D**   1966

Question 4   Which of the following statements is correct?

☐ **A**   The 'Swinging Sixties' are a famous British rock band.

☐ **B**   The 'Swinging Sixties' are associated with a period of social change in the 1960s.

Question 5   Is the statement below ☐ TRUE or ☐ FALSE?

Many of the great thinkers of the Enlightenment were Scottish.

Question 6   Which TWO are British inventions of the 20th century?

☐ **A**   Diesel engines

☐ **B**   World Wide Web

☐ **C**   Steam trains

☐ **D**   Hovercraft

Question 7   Why is the Habeas Corpus Act of 1679 so important?

☐ **A**   It guaranteed no one could be held prisoner unlawfully.

☐ **B**   It introduced the registration of cemeteries.

☐ **C**   It ensured the right to a proper funeral.

☐ **D**   It ended capital punishment in the UK.

Question 8   Is the statement below ☐ TRUE or ☐ FALSE?

During the reign of Queen Victoria, the British Empire became the largest empire the world has ever seen.

Question 9   What was an important achievement of King James I?

☐ **A**   He won a civil war against the monarchy.

☐ **B**   He authorised a new translation of the Bible into English.

☐ **C**   He defeated an invasion of the Spanish Armada.

☐ **D**   He reformed the Catholic Church in England.

Question 10   Who was the first British Prime Minister?

☐ **A**   Sir Kingsley Amis

☐ **B**   Sir Ian Botham

☐ **C**   Sir Winston Churchill

☐ **D**   Sir Robert Walpole

Question 11 Which of the following statements is correct?

☐ **A** The Bill of Rights in 1689 confirmed the rights of Parliament and the limits of the king's power.

☐ **B** The Bill of Rights in 1689 outlined the human rights of British citizens.

Question 12 Which TWO did the Romans introduce to Britain?

☐ **A** A structure of law

☐ **B** Plants and animals

☐ **C** Metal working

☐ **D** The Magna Carta

Question 13 Is the statement below ☐ TRUE or ☐ FALSE?

In 1588 the English defeated a large French fleet of ships that intended to land an army in England.

Question 14 Hadrian's Wall was built to keep out which group of people?

☐ **A** The French

☐ **B** The Welsh

☐ **C** The Picts

☐ **D** The Vikings

Question 15 Which of the following statements is correct?

☐ **A** The Industrial Revolution was a protest by factory workers in the 1980s.

☐ **B** The Industrial Revolution was the rapid development of industry that took place in the 18th and 19th centuries.

Question 16 What did the Education Act of 1944 introduce?

☐ **A** Compulsory education up to the age of 18

☐ **B** Air-conditioning facilities in all schools

☐ **C** Free secondary education in England and Wales

☐ **D** Free milk for children under 12

Question 17 Is the statement below ☐ TRUE or ☐ FALSE?

The civil war between King Charles I and Parliament in the mid-17th century led to Oliver Cromwell being crowned king of England.

Question 18 Which of the following statements is correct?

☐ **A** When William of Orange invaded England in 1688, he proclaimed himself king and met no resistance.

☐ **B** When William of Orange invaded England in 1688, it sparked the Hundred Years War.

Question 19 Is the statement below ☐ TRUE or ☐ FALSE?

'The Battle of Britain' was an aerial battle against the Germans during the Second World War.

Question 20 Which TWO things is Queen Elizabeth I's reign remembered for?

☐ **A** The Great Fire of London

☐ **B** Winning the Wars of the Roses

☐ **C** English settlers colonising the eastern coast of America

☐ **D** Poetry and drama, especially the work of Shakespeare

Answers and pointers to questions

Question	Answer	Explanation	Page reference in *Life in the United Kingdom: A Guide for New Residents*
1	A and D	The Reform Act of 1832 greatly increased the number of people with the right to vote. More parliamentary seats were given to towns and cities. The Act also abolished the old pocket and rotten boroughs.	Page 50
2	A	Britain (with Turkey and France) fought against Russia in the Crimean War (1853–6).	Page 49
3	B	In 1918, women over the age of 30 were given the right to vote. (In 1928, women were given the right to vote at the age of 21, the same as men.)	Page 51
4	B	The decade of the 1960s was a period of significant social change and known as the 'Swinging Sixties'. There was growth in British fashion, cinema and popular music.	Page 63
5	TRUE	Adam Smith developed ideas about economics. David Hume's ideas about human nature continue to influence philosophers. James Watt's work on steam power helped the progress of the Industrial Revolution.	Page 40
6	B and D	The World Wide Web was invented by Sir Tim Berners-Lee, and information was transmitted via the web for the first time on 25 December 1990. Sir Christopher Cockerell invented the hovercraft in the 1950s.	Pages 64–5
7	A	The Habeas Corpus Act of 1679 guaranteed no one could be held prisoner unlawfully. This legislation remains relevant today, and every prisoner has a right to a court hearing.	Page 35

Question	Answer	Explanation	Page reference in *Life in the United Kingdom: A Guide for New Residents*
8	TRUE	During the reign of Queen Victoria, the British Empire grew to cover India, Australia and large parts of Africa. It became the largest empire the world has ever seen, with an estimated population of 400 million people.	Page 47
9	B	James I authorised a new translation of the Bible into English. The translation is known as the 'King James Version' or the 'Authorised Version'.	Page 31
10	D	During George I's reign the most important minister in Parliament became known as the Prime Minister. Sir Robert Walpole was the first British Prime Minister, from 1721 to 1742.	Page 39
11	A	The Bill of Rights in 1689 confirmed the rights of Parliament and the limits of the king's power. The balance of power between monarch and Parliament had now permanently changed.	Page 37
12	A and B	The Romans occupied Britain for 400 years. They built roads and public buildings, created a structure of law, and introduced new plants and animals to Britain.	Page 17
13	FALSE	In 1588, during the reign of Elizabeth I, the English defeated the Spanish Armada (a large fleet of ships), which had been sent by Spain to conquer England and restore Catholicism.	Page 29
14	C	During the Roman occupation of Britain, Emperor Hadrian built a wall in the north of England to keep out the Picts (ancestors of the Scottish people). Parts of the wall can still be seen today.	Page 17

Question	Answer	Explanation	Page reference in *Life in the United Kingdom: A Guide for New Residents*
15	B	The Industrial Revolution was the rapid development of industry that took place in the 18th and 19th centuries. Britain was the first country to industrialise on a large scale.	Page 40
16	C	R A Butler oversaw the Education Act of 1944 (often called the 'Butler Act'), which introduced free secondary education in England and Wales.	Page 62
17	FALSE	After the English Civil War, Charles I was executed and England became a republic. Oliver Cromwell was recognised as leader of the new republic, and was given the title of Lord Protector.	Pages 33–4
18	A	In 1688, important Protestants in England asked William of Orange to invade England and proclaim himself king in place of James II. There was no resistance, and the event was later called the 'Glorious Revolution'.	Page 36
19	TRUE	During the Second World War, Germany waged an air campaign against Britain, but the British resisted with their fighter planes and eventually won the aerial battle, called 'the Battle of Britain'.	Page 58
20	C and D	During Elizabeth I's reign, English settlers first began to colonise the eastern coast of America. The Elizabethan period is also remembered for the richness of its poetry and drama, especially the plays and poems of William Shakespeare.	Pages 29–30

A modern, thriving society

Cities of the UK

1. London
2. Birmingham
3. Liverpool
4. Leeds
5. Sheffield
6. Bristol
7. Manchester
8. Bradford
9. Newcastle upon Tyne
10. Plymouth
11. Southampton
12. Norwich
13. Cardiff
14. Swansea
15. Newport
16. Belfast
17. Edinburgh
18. Glasgow
19. Dundee
20. Aberdeen

Capital cities

The capital city of the UK is London

Scotland
The capital city of Scotland is Edinburgh

Wales
The capital city of Wales is Cardiff

Northern Ireland
The capital city of Northern Ireland is Belfast

England

Wales

Northern Ireland

Scotland

Orkney Isles

Shetland Islands

Find out ...

✓ Where is the UK located in Europe?

✓ What is the longest distance on the mainland of the UK?

✓ Name five cities in England, apart from the capital.

✓ Name two cities in Scotland, apart from the capital.

✓ Name one city in Wales, apart from the capital.

The UK today

Currency

The currency of the UK is pound sterling (symbol £). There are 100 pence in a pound.

Coins are of the following values: 1p, 2p, 5p, 10p, 20p, 50p, £1 and £2.

Notes are of the following values: £5, £10, £20, £50.

The currency of the UK is pound sterling

Northern Ireland and Scotland use the same pounds and pence but have their own banknotes. These banknotes are valid everywhere but do not have to be accepted in shops.

Languages and dialects

Everyone in the UK speaks English but there are also regional languages and dialects.

Country	Language
Wales	Welsh is taught in schools
Scotland	Some Gaelic
Northern Ireland	Some Irish Gaelic

Find out ...

✓ What languages are spoken in the countries of the UK?

✓ Where in Scotland is Gaelic spoken?

Population

The population of the UK has grown steadily since the 15th century

Year	Population
1600	Just over 4 million
1700	5 million
1801	8 million
1851	20 million
1901	40 million
1951	50 million
1998	57 million
2005	Just under 60 million
2010	Just over 62 million

Source: National Statistics

The population is unequally divided between the four countries which make up the UK

England	84%
Scotland	8%
Wales	5%
Northern Ireland	3%

The UK population is ageing because there is a better standard of living and healthcare

There are now more people aged 85 or more than ever before

Ethnicity

The biggest group of people in the UK is white. This includes people from Europe, Australia, Canada, New Zealand and the United States. Other significant groups are Asian, black and mixed descent.

Find out ...

✓ How is the population of the UK changing?

An equal society

In the UK, men and women have equal rights to work, own property, marry and divorce. If they are married, both parents are equally responsible for their children.

Women in Britain today:

- make up about half of the workforce
- on average leave school with better qualifications than boys
- make up more than half of the university population
- work in all sectors of the economy
- are in more high-level positions than ever before
- often continue to work after having children.

In many families today, both partners work and both share responsibility for childcare and household chores.

Find out ...

✓ How has the role of women changed in UK society?

Religion

Historically, the UK is a Christian country but everyone is free to choose their own religion.

The Church of England

- A Protestant church
- The official church of the state in England
- The head of the church is the monarch
- The Archbishop of Canterbury is the spiritual leader
- The monarch, with the guidance of the Prime Minister, chooses the Archbishop
- Some bishops sit in the House of Lords

The Church of Scotland

- A Protestant, Presbyterian church
- The Moderator often speaks on behalf of the church
- Organised by the General Assembly of the Church of Scotland

Wales and Northern Ireland have no established church.

Other Protestant Christian groups in the UK include Baptists, Presbyterians, Methodists and Quakers. Roman Catholics form the biggest non-Protestant Christian denomination.

Patron saints

Each country in the UK has a patron saint with a special day.

Wales: St David's Day, 1 March

Northern Ireland: St Patrick's Day, 17 March

England: St George's Day, 23 April

Scotland: St Andrew's Day, 30 November

Find out …

- ✓ What religions are followed in the UK?
- ✓ What are the different religious buildings called?
- ✓ Do Wales and Northern Island have established churches?
- ✓ Are patron saints' days national holidays?

Customs and traditions

Christian festivals

Christmas Day, 25 December, marks the birth of Jesus Christ. Many Christians go to church and families get together to celebrate. They eat a special meal which often includes turkey, Christmas pudding and mince pies. Children love Christmas because everyone exchanges presents, people decorate their houses with Christmas trees and 'Father Christmas' leaves presents for them.

Boxing Day on 26 December is a public holiday.

Easter takes place in March or April. Good Friday and Easter Sunday mark the death and resurrection of Jesus Christ. Good Friday and Easter Monday are public holidays.

Other religious festivals

Diwali is celebrated by Hindus and Sikhs in October or November. It celebrates the victory of good over evil and the gaining of knowledge.

Hannukah is celebrated by Jews in November or December. It marks the Jews' struggle for religious freedom.

Eid al-Fitr is celebrated by Muslims to mark the end of the month's fast during Ramadan. They thank Allah for giving them the strength to complete the fast.

Eid ul Adha remembers that the prophet Ibrahim was willing to sacrifice his son when God ordered him to.

Vaisakhi (also spelled Baisakhi) is a Sikh festival which celebrates the founding of the Sikh community known as the Khalsa. It is celebrated on 14 April each year with parades, dancing and singing.

Find out ...

✓ What festivals are celebrated by the main religions of the UK?

✓   What are bank holidays and when do they take place?

✓ Why is 11 November important? How is it commemorated?

✓ What do Valentine's Day and Bonfire Night each represent?

Festivals in the UK

1 January

New Year's Day is a public holiday. People usually celebrate on the night of 31 December. In Scotland, 31 December is called Hogmanay and 2 January is also a public holiday.

14 February

Valentine's Day is when lovers exchange cards and gifts. Sometimes people receive cards from secret admirers.

March–April

Mothering Sunday (or Mother's Day) is the Sunday three weeks before Easter. Children give their mothers cards and presents.

March–April

Easter celebrates the death and resurrection of Jesus Christ.

1 April

April Fool's Day is when people play jokes on each other until midday. The television and newspapers often have stories that are April Fool jokes.

June

Father's Day is the third Sunday in June, when children give their fathers cards and presents.

There are also several days during the year when people have a holiday from work. These are known as bank holidays.

31 October

Halloween is when young people often dress up in frightening costumes to play 'trick or treat'. People carve lanterns out of pumpkins and put a candle inside.

5 November

Bonfire Night is when people in Great Britain set off fireworks at home or in special displays. The origin of this celebration was an event in 1605, when a group of Catholics led by Guy Fawkes failed in their plan to kill the Protestant king with a bomb in the Houses of Parliament.

11 November

Remembrance Day commemorates those who died fighting in the First World War, Second World War and other wars.

25 December

Christmas Day celebrates the birth of Jesus Christ

Sport

Football

Football is the UK's most popular sport. England, Scotland, Wales and Northern Ireland each have separate leagues and their own national team. The English Premier League attracts a huge international audience. People all over the country play in amateur teams, just for fun.

Rugby

Rugby union and rugby league are both played in the UK. Teams from all four countries compete in national and international competitions. Amateur teams play in regional leagues.

Horse racing
There are racecourses all over the UK. Famous horse-racing events include Royal Ascot, the Grand National and the Scottish Grand National at Ayr.

Tennis

Tennis is widely played across the UK. The Wimbledon Championships are world-famous.

People play and watch many sports in the UK

Cricket

There are amateur and professional cricket teams across the UK. The most famous competition is the Ashes, which is a series of matches played between England and Australia each year.

Water sports
Both rowing and sailing are popular leisure and competitive activities.

Motor sports
The UK is a leader in the development of motor-sport technology and racing. A Grand Prix is held here every year.

Skiing

Many people go abroad to ski, but you can ski in Scotland in the winter.

Golf

Golf is a popular sport played socially and professionally. There are golf courses all over the UK. The Open Championship is an international competition that takes place every year.

Find out …

✓ When have the Olympics been held in the UK?

✓ How did the Paralympic Games originate?

✓ Who provides sports facilities in the UK?

✓ Name some famous British sports men and women.

✓ Which is the most popular sport in the UK?

✓ Name some famous sporting events in the UK.

Arts and culture

Music

Classical and pop music play an important role in British society.

A series of classical concerts, known as the Proms, takes place in London every summer.

Music events, both classic and popular, occur at venues such as Wembley Stadium, The O2 in London and the Scottish Exhibition and Conference Centre in Glasgow.

Every summer there are festivals across the UK. Glastonbury, the Isle of Wight, the V Festival and many others offer the chance to hear famous and up-and-coming bands and singers.

The Mercury Music Prize is awarded for the best album from the UK and Ireland. The Brit Awards celebrate the best of British popular music.

The National Eisteddfod of Wales includes music, dance, art and original performances, largely in Welsh.

Find out ...

✓ Which famous composers have lived and worked in the UK, and what are their best-known works?

✓ What other sorts of music are popular in the UK?

✓ Which famous bands have influenced pop music in the UK and abroad?

Theatre

There are theatres in most towns and cities throughout the UK, ranging from the large to the small. Plays and musicals are performed by both professional and amateur companies. There are many theatres in London's West End.

The Edinburgh Festival is held every summer, and includes art, theatre and music events. 'The Fringe' is part of the festival, offering experimental work and comedy.

The Laurence Olivier Awards celebrate the best of British theatre. They are named after the British actor Laurence Olivier, who was famous for his Shakespearean roles.

Street performers at the Edinburgh Festival

Find out ...

✓ Which composers have written comic operas and musicals?

✓ What is pantomime?

Art

Works by British and international artists are displayed in galleries across the UK. Some of the most well-known galleries are The National Gallery and Tate Modern in London, the National Museum in Cardiff and the National Gallery of Scotland in Edinburgh.

The Turner Prize is given for contemporary art. It is recognised as one of the most prestigious awards in Europe. Winners include Damien Hirst and Richard Wright.

Find out ...

✓ What trends have there been in art in the UK?

✓ Name some famous British artists and their work.

Architecture

The UK has many churches, cathedrals and castles from the Middle Ages and Norman periods.

As the country became more peaceful, great country houses and other buildings were erected in the distinctive styles of each era.

Find out ...

✓ Name a style of architecture from each century since the Middle Ages.

✓ Which architect and gardener worked together on their designs?

✓ Name some modern British architects who have been responsible for major design projects.

Architectural styles in the UK

17th century
Famous architects included Inigo Jones and Sir Christopher Wren

Queen's House, Greenwich
Architect: Inigo Jones
Style: Classical

St Paul's Cathedral, London
Architect: Sir Christopher Wren
Style: English Baroque

18th century
Robert Adam's elegant designs became popular

Dumfries House, Scotland
Architect: Robert Adam
Style: Palladian

Harewood House, Leeds
Architects: John Carr, Robert Adam
Type: stately home

19th century
The medieval 'gothic' style was favoured during this century

Houses of Parliament
Architect: Charles Barry
Style: Perpendicular Gothic

St Pancras railway station (front)
Architect: George Gilbert Scott
Style: Victorian Gothic

20th century
Modern British architects include Sir Norman Foster, Lord Richard Rogers and Dame Zaha Hadid

The Cenotaph, Whitehall
Architect: Sir Edwin Lutyens
Construction: Portland stone

30 St Mary Axe, London (also known as the Gherkin)
Architect: Sir Norman Foster
Style: modern

Landscaping and garden design

Alongside architecture, garden design has also been important in the UK. 'Capability' Brown created landscaped gardens around country houses in the 18th century, and later Gertrude Jekyll collaborated with Edwin Lutyens to create colourful gardens around the houses he designed.

Fashion and design

Britain has produced many great designers, from Thomas Chippendale (who designed furniture in the 18th century) to Clarice Cliff (who designed Art Deco ceramics) to Sir Terence Conran (a 20th-century interior designer). Leading fashion designers of recent years include Mary Quant, Alexander McQueen and Vivienne Westwood.

Literature

Many famous authors have emerged from the UK. The Man Booker Prize for Fiction is awarded annually for the best novel written by an author from the Commonwealth, Ireland or Zimbabwe. Winners include Ian McEwan, Hilary Mantel and Julian Barnes. Several British authors have won the Nobel Prize in Literature. There is also a great deal of popular literature which is read all over the world.

Find out ...

✓ Name some of the British authors who have won the Nobel Prize in Literature.

✓ Name some notable UK authors and some of the books they have written.

Poets

British poetry has a long tradition, stretching from the time of the Anglo-Saxons right up until the present day.

Poets' Corner in Westminster Abbey commemorates the work of many UK poets.

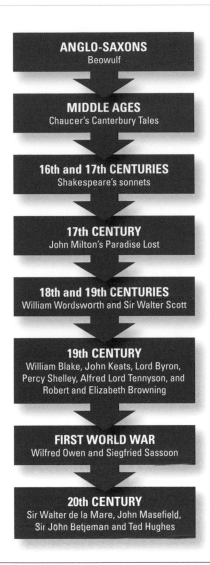

ANGLO-SAXONS
Beowulf

MIDDLE AGES
Chaucer's Canterbury Tales

16th and 17th CENTURIES
Shakespeare's sonnets

17th CENTURY
John Milton's Paradise Lost

18th and 19th CENTURIES
William Wordsworth and Sir Walter Scott

19th CENTURY
William Blake, John Keats, Lord Byron,
Percy Shelley, Alfred Lord Tennyson, and
Robert and Elizabeth Browning

FIRST WORLD WAR
Wilfred Owen and Siegfried Sassoon

20th CENTURY
Sir Walter de la Mare, John Masefield,
Sir John Betjeman and Ted Hughes

Find out ...

✓ For each century since the Middle Ages, find some examples of poetry written by famous poets of the UK.

✓ Explain the inspiration for some of their writing.

✓ What famous lines were written by Robert Browning, Lord Byron, William Blake and Wilfred Owen?

Places of interest

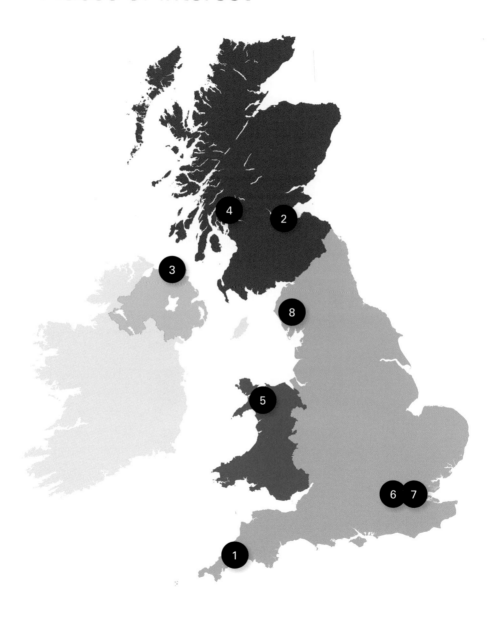

1. The Eden Project

The Eden Project shows plants from all over the world in its biomes (giant greenhouses).

5. Snowdonia

This national park covers an area of 2,170 square kilometres. Snowdon is the highest mountain in Wales.

2. Edinburgh Castle

The castle sits on a rock overlooking Edinburgh.

6. London Eye

This Ferris wheel is 135 metres tall. It was built as part of the UK's celebration of the new millennium.

3. The Giant's Causeway

This is a land formation of columns made from volcanic lava. It was formed about 50 million years ago.

7. The Tower of London

William the Conqueror built the Tower after he became king in 1066. Beefeaters show visitors the Tower. The Crown Jewels are also on show.

4. Loch Lomond and the Trossachs

This national park covers 1,865 square kilometres. Loch Lomond is the largest expanse of fresh water in mainland Britain.

8. The Lake District

The Lake District is England's largest national park. It is famous for its lakes and mountains and is very popular with climbers, walkers and sailors.

Find out ...

✓ Name a place of interest in England, Wales, Scotland and Northern Ireland and explain why each one is famous.

✓ Which places of interest have historical connections and which are natural environments?

Leisure

People spend their free time in many different ways.

Around the home

Television and radio

There are many different television channels. People enjoy watching soap operas, drama and sport. If you have a television, you need a licence which pays for the BBC. There are many different radio stations offering a wide range of material. Some radio and television stations broadcast in regional languages.

Social networking

People use networking websites such as Facebook and Twitter to voice opinions, follow events and news, and keep in touch with friends and family.

Cooking and entertaining

People often entertain at home, inviting friends round for a meal. Television chefs have made cooking a popular pastime.

Pets

Many people have dogs, cats and other pet animals at home. They must be kept under control and it is wise to have them vaccinated against common diseases.

Gardening

Houses often have gardens and people enjoy growing flowers and vegetables. Some people also rent an allotment to give them more space for growing food crops. There are many beautiful gardens which are open to the public.

Find out ...

✓ Who needs a TV licence?

✓ Name some gardens which are open to the public.

✓ Name the national flowers of each country in the UK.

✓ What regional dishes are cooked in the UK?

✓ What responsibilities does the owner of a dog have?

Out and about

Pubs and nightclubs

Pubs are found all over the country in towns and villages. You must be 18 or over to drink alcohol in a pub. Clubs are usually in city centres and are open late into the night.

Films

The British film industry has had an important influence on modern cinema. Many famous films have been made in the UK. British actors have worked in both the UK and Hollywood and many have won Oscars and BAFTAs, the UK equivalent.

Comedy

Both comedy and satire have always played a part in British life. Medieval kings had jesters who made fun of people in the court. Shakespeare wrote comic plays and cartoonists ridiculed people in the public eye.

Today people go out to see comedians and watch comedy programmes on the television.

Betting and gambling

In betting shops and casinos you can gamble on sports and games. You have to be 18 or over to go in. People also buy lottery tickets and scratch cards to try to win money.

Shopping

Town centres and shopping malls both offer extensive opportunities for shopping. Shops are often open seven days a week.

Find out ...

✓ How has the UK film industry developed?

✓ Name some famous films made in the UK.

✓ Name some British actors who have won Oscars.

✓ How has comedy developed in the UK?

✓ Name some comedians and comedy programmes on British television.

✓ How does the law affect people's pastimes, such as betting, gambling and drinking?

Practice questions

Question 1   Is the statement below ☐ TRUE or ☐ FALSE?

The Turner Prize is awarded for the best new novel of the year.

Question 2   Which TWO facts relate to the UK's national heritage?

☐ **A**   There are 25 national parks in England, Scotland and Wales.

☐ **B**   All national parks are run by the National Trust.

☐ **C**   There are 15 national parks in England, Scotland and Wales.

☐ **D**   The National Trust is a charity that maintains much land and many historic properties.

Question 3   Who is the patron saint of England?

☐ **A**   St David

☐ **B**   St George

☐ **C**   St Patrick

☐ **D**   St Andrew

Question 4   Which of the following statements is correct?

☐ **A**   People under the age of 18 are not allowed to participate in the National Lottery.

☐ **B**   People under the age of 16 are not allowed to participate in the National Lottery.

Question 5   Is the statement below ☐ TRUE or ☐ FALSE?

Many communities have a local 'pub' that is a natural focal point for social activities.

Question 6   Which of the following statements is correct?

     ☐ **A**   The Ashes is a series of cricket matches played between England and Australia.

     ☐ **B**   The Grand National is a major UK motor-racing event.

Question 7   Which TWO dates are public holidays in England?

     ☐ **A**   1 January

     ☐ **B**   2 January

     ☐ **C**   31 October

     ☐ **D**   26 December

Question 8   What type of sporting event is the Grand National?

     ☐ **A**   Tennis tournament

     ☐ **B**   Golf championship

     ☐ **C**   Football match

     ☐ **D**   Horse race

Question 9   Which of the following statements is correct?

     ☐ **A**   Baptists and Methodists are Christian groups linked to the Roman Catholic Church.

     ☐ **B**   Baptists and Methodists are Protestant Christian groups.

Question 10   Is the statement below ☐ TRUE or ☐ FALSE?

Four Weddings and a Funeral *and* Brief Encounter
are famous British films.

Question 11 In what part of the UK is Hogmanay traditionally celebrated?

☐ **A** Scotland

☐ **B** England

☐ **C** Wales

☐ **D** Northern Ireland

Question 12 Which TWO are famous British sports people?

☐ **A** Kate Winslet

☐ **B** David Weir

☐ **C** John Petts

☐ **D** Bobby Moore

Question 13 Which of the following statements is correct?

☐ **A** Money from TV licences is used to pay for all TV services.

☐ **B** Money from TV licences is used to pay for the British Broadcasting Corporation (BBC).

Question 14 Which TWO are famous British artists?

☐ **A** Thomas Gainsborough

☐ **B** Sir John Lavery

☐ **C** Benjamin Britten

☐ **D** Graham Greene

Question 15 Is the statement below ☐ TRUE or ☐ FALSE?

People still speak forms of the Gaelic language in Scotland and Ireland.

Question 16 Which TWO points about regional foods are correct?

☐ **A** Scotland is well known for haggis, which is made from chicken.

☐ **B** Scotland is well known for haggis, which is made from a sheep's stomach.

☐ **C** Fish and tomatoes is a well-known English dish.

☐ **D** The ingredients of Welsh cakes include dried fruits, spices and flour.

Question 17 What activity is associated with Facebook and Twitter?

☐ **A** Book clubs

☐ **B** Farming

☐ **C** Social networking

☐ **D** Online discount stores

Question 18 Is the statement below ☐ TRUE or ☐ FALSE?

In Britain, the local council is responsible for cleaning up after people's dogs in public places.

Question 19 Which of the following statements is correct?

☐ **A** The thistle is the national flower of Scotland.

☐ **B** The daffodil is the national flower of Scotland.

Question 20 Which TWO are buildings designed by the 17th-century architect Inigo Jones?

☐ **A** Durham Cathedral

☐ **B** Queen's House at Greenwich

☐ **C** Banqueting House in Whitehall

☐ **D** The Tower of London

Answers and pointers to questions

Question	Answer	Explanation	Page reference in *Life in the United Kingdom: A Guide for New Residents*
1	FALSE	The Turner Prize was established in 1984 and celebrates contemporary art.	Page 95
2	C and D	There are 15 national parks in England, Scotland and Wales. The National Trust in England, Wales and Northern Ireland, and the National Trust for Scotland, are charities that work to preserve important buildings, coastline and countryside.	Page 107
3	B	St George is the patron saint of England, and St George's Day is celebrated on 23 April each year.	Page 77
4	B	People under 16 are not allowed to participate in the National Lottery.	Pages 106–7
5	TRUE	Pubs, or public houses, are an important part of the UK social culture.	Page 106
6	A	The most famous competition in British cricket is the Ashes, which is a series of Test matches played between England and Australia.	Page 87
7	A and D	1 January is New Year's Day and 26 December is Boxing Day. Both are public holidays, which means shops and businesses usually close for the day.	Pages 80 and 82
8	D	The Grand National is a famous horse-racing event that takes place each year at Aintree near Liverpool.	Page 88
9	B	Baptists and Methodists are both Protestant Christian groups.	Page 77

Question	Answer	Explanation	Page reference in *Life in the United Kingdom: A Guide for New Residents*
10	TRUE	*Brief Encounter* was released in 1945 and was directed by David Lean. *Four Weddings and a Funeral* was released in 1994 and was directed by Mike Newell.	Page 104
11	A	31 December, New Year's Eve, is called Hogmanay in Scotland.	Page 82
12	B and D	David Weir is a Paralympian who uses a wheelchair, and has won six gold medals over two Paralympic Games. Bobby Moore captained the English football team that won the World Cup in 1966.	Pages 85–6
13	B	The money from TV licences is used to pay for the British Broadcasting Corporation (BBC). This is a British public service broadcaster providing television and radio programmes.	Pages 105–6
14	A and B	Thomas Gainsborough (1727–88) and Sir John Lavery (1856–1941) were British portrait painters.	Page 94
15	TRUE	In Scotland, Gaelic is spoken in some parts of the Highlands and Islands, and in Northern Ireland some people speak Irish Gaelic.	Page 74
16	B and D	A traditional food in Scotland is haggis, which is a sheep's stomach stuffed with offal, suet, onions and oatmeal. Welsh cakes are a traditional Welsh snack made from flour, dried fruits and spices.	Page 102
17	C	Social networking sites such as Facebook and Twitter are a popular way for people to stay in touch with friends.	Page 106

Question	Answer	Explanation	Page reference in *Life in the United Kingdom: A Guide for New Residents*
18	FALSE	In the UK, dog owners are responsible for cleaning up after their dog in a public place.	Page 107
19	A	The thistle is the national flower of Scotland.	Page 101
20	B and C	In the 17th century, Inigo Jones took inspiration from classical architecture to design the Queen's House at Greenwich and the Banqueting House in Whitehall in London.	Page 96

The UK government,
the law and your role

- The development of British democracy
- The British constitution
- The government
- The UK and international institutions

- Respecting the law
- The role of the courts
- Fundamental principles
- Taxation
- Driving

- Your role in the community
- How you can support your community
- Looking after the environment

The development of British democracy

The UK is a Parliamentary democracy. Since 1969, the voting age has been 18. Over the previous hundred years an increasing number of people had been given the vote and it was no longer restricted to the male aristocracy. Women achieved the vote after a long campaign by the suffragettes.

The British constitution

The British constitution is not written down as it is in the United States. It is a set of principles and institutions that are the basis of how the country is run. Most of the rest of this section explains the workings of the constitution.

The monarch gives advice but does not make political decisions. This is known as a constitutional monarchy. The government is elected by the people, but after a General Election the new Prime Minister will go to see the monarch to be sworn in.

Queen Elizabeth II has reigned since her father's death in 1952. Her oldest son, Prince Charles (the Prince of Wales), is the heir to the throne.

The National Anthem celebrates the role of the monarch and new citizens swear allegiance to the monarch as part of the citizenship ceremony.

Parliament is composed of:

- the House of Commons, which is fully elected
- the House of Lords, which is a mix of people who have been selected by the political parties and those who have hereditary rights.

The Houses of Parliament in Westminster, London, where the House of Commons and the House of Lords sit

The House of Commons is made up of members of Parliament (MPs) who are elected to represent regions of the country, known as constituencies. Most MPs represent a political party and the party with most MPs forms the government. If there isn't a majority, parties may join together and form a coalition. MPs represent all the people in their constituency – not just those who have voted for them. Their main role is to scrutinise and pass laws. The Speaker is an MP chosen by MPs to chair the House of Commons.

The chamber of the House of Commons

No parliament can last for more than five years – a law which aims to protect democracy.

Find out ...

✓ How and when did the UK become a full democracy?

✓ What is the role of the monarch?

The chamber of the House of Lords

The House of Lords checks and amends legislation but has less power than the House of Commons.

Find out ...

✓ What is the difference between the House of Commons and the House of Lords?

✓ What system is used to elect MPs?

✓ What happens if an MP resigns or dies?

✓ What can happen if no party wins a majority?

✓ How can you contact your MP?

The government

The government is led by the Prime Minister, who lives at 10 Downing Street. He or she appoints the cabinet, which is the inner group of ministers who take prime responsibility for government policy. The Chancellor of the Exchequer runs the Treasury, the Home Secretary is responsible for home affairs and the Foreign Secretary is in charge of foreign affairs. Secretaries of State are in charge of all the other areas.

The opposition is made up of the MPs belonging to the losing political parties. The leader of the biggest party appoints a shadow cabinet to challenge the government.

The party system is made up of the parties involved in British politics. These include the Labour Party, the Conservative Party, the Liberal Democrats, or one of the parties representing Scottish, Welsh or Northern Irish interests.

MPs can be elected as 'independents'. Independent MPs usually represent an issue important to their constituency.

Individuals can join political parties if they want to support their work.

Pressure and lobby groups try to influence government policy. There are many pressure groups in the UK. Some represent economic groupings and others are concerned about issues such as the environment.

The civil service develops and carries out government policy. Appointments to the civil service are not political. Staff must have integrity, honesty, objectivity and impartiality (including being politically neutral).

Local government runs many aspects of services in local communities. Local councils are elected. They are usually led by a mayor who is either appointed by councillors or elected by the community. London, for example has an elected mayor. Councillors normally represent a political party.

The money to pay for local services comes from central government and local taxes.

Find out …

✓   Which are the main political parties?

✓   What do pressure groups try to do?

✓   How is a mayor appointed?

✓   Where does the money come from to pay for local services?

Devolved administrations were established in the late 1990s. The Welsh Assembly and the Scottish Parliament were set up in 1999. The Northern Ireland Parliament was established in 1922, but the Northern Ireland Assembly was not set up until later (in 1998).

Policy and laws governing defence, foreign affairs, immigration, taxation and social security all remain under central UK government control. The Scottish Parliament has more power than the Welsh and Northern Ireland Assemblies.

The UK government has the power to suspend all devolved assemblies. It has used this power several times in Northern Ireland when local political leaders found it difficult to work together. However, the Assembly has been running successfully since 2007.

Find out …

✓   What are the powers of the Welsh and Northern Ireland Assemblies and the Scottish Parliament?

✓   How would you go about visiting the parliaments of the UK?

The media and government

Everything said in Parliament is published in *Hansard*, which is available online the next day. There is also a TV channel which shows parliamentary proceedings live.

The UK has a free press. Sometimes newspapers run campaigns to persuade the government to change the law. Radio and television coverage of political parties must be balanced and they must be given equal time.

Find out ...

✓ How can you find out what is going on in Parliament?

✓ What is meant by 'a free press'?

Who can vote?

Elections are held for local government, national government and the European Parliament. Almost all British and Commonwealth citizens over the age of 18 can vote as long as they are on the electoral register. Every household is sent a form to complete to be included in the register. Voting takes place in polling stations which might be in a local school or community hall. EU citizens living in the UK can vote in local elections but not General Elections. Most citizens of the UK, Irish Republic and Commonwealth can stand for election to the national Parliament or the local council.

Find out ...

✓ Can EU citizens of other countries vote in General Elections?

✓ How can you ensure that you are on the electoral register?

✓ How does the voting system differ in Northern Ireland?

✓ How do you vote on election day?

✓ How do you vote if you can't be there on election day?

The UK and international institutions

The Commonwealth

The Commonwealth is a group of 53 countries. Most were originally members of the British Empire. A few other countries have joined. It is based on the core values of democracy, good government and the rule of law.

The Queen is head of the Commonwealth. The organisation has no power over its members, apart from suspending membership.

> ## Find out …
> ✓ Which countries are members of the Commonwealth?
> ✓ What does the Commonwealth do?

The European Union

The UK joined the European Union (EU) in 1973. When the European Economic Community was originally set up in 1957, the UK decided not to join. There are now 27 member countries and Croatia will join in 2013.

The Council of Europe

The Council of Europe is separate from the EU. It is responsible for the protection and promotion of human rights. It developed the European Convention on Human Rights which has been incorporated into the UK's Human Rights Act.

Find out ...

✓ What is the difference between the European Union and the Council of Europe?

✓ How do EU laws affect the UK?

The United Nations

The UK is part of the United Nations (UN), an international organisation with more than 190 countries as members. It was set up after the Second World War, and aims to prevent war and promote international peace and security.

The UN Security Council has 15 members. The UK is one of the five permanent members. The Security Council decides how international crises should be dealt with.

The North Atlantic Treaty Organization

The UK is a member of the North Atlantic Treaty Organization (NATO), which was set up to help member countries defend themselves. The 28 member countries all have an equal say in decision-making.

Find out ...

✓ Why was the United Nations set up?

✓ What are its main objectives?

✓ Why was NATO established?

Respecting the law

People's legal responsibilities in the UK are set out in law. Everyone, regardless of their background, is expected to obey the law and to understand that some things which may be allowed in other countries are not acceptable in the UK. People who do not respect the law should not expect to be allowed to become permanent residents in the UK.

Everyone has the right to equal treatment – whoever they are and wherever they come from.

The law in the UK

There are two types of law, criminal and civil.

Crimes such as murder, theft and assault are dealt with under criminal law, as in most other countries. You can find out more about types of crime in the UK at www.gov.uk.

Carrying a weapon

Anti-social behaviour

Selling tobacco to anyone under the age of 18

Using abusive language or harassing someone because of their religion or ethnic origin

CRIMINAL LAW
Breaking criminal law is an offence which usually involves the police

Smoking in public places

Selling and buying drugs

Selling alcohol to anyone who is under the age of 18

Some places have alcohol-free zones where you cannot drink in public

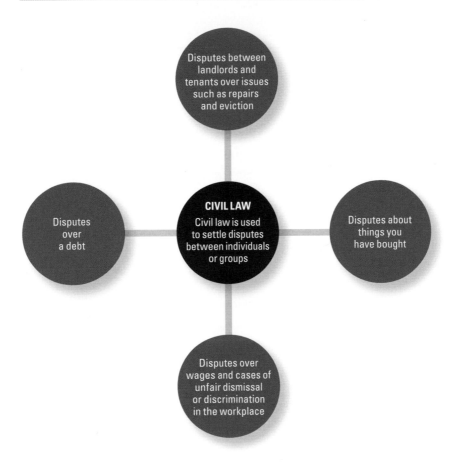

Disputes between landlords and tenants over issues such as repairs and eviction

Disputes over a debt

CIVIL LAW
Civil law is used to settle disputes between individuals or groups

Disputes about things you have bought

Disputes over wages and cases of unfair dismissal or discrimination in the workplace

Find out ...

✓ How are people treated by the law in the UK?

✓ What is the difference between criminal law and civil law?

✓ Give some examples of criminal law and civil law.

✓ Where can you find out more about the law?

The police

Policing is a public service that helps and protects everyone, no matter what their background or where they live. It is independent of government.

The police:

- protect life and property
- prevent disturbances
- prevent and detect crime.

Police officers are supported by police community support officers (PCSOs). All police officers must obey the law. Corrupt police officers are severely punished.

From November 2012 the public have elected Police and Crime Commissioners (PCCs) in England and Wales to be responsible for the effective running of police in their area.

Everyone is expected to help the police prevent and detect crimes. If you are arrested and taken to a police station, a police officer will tell you the reason for your arrest and you will be able to seek legal advice.

If you think you have not been treated properly by the police, you can make a complaint.

Terrorism and extremism

The UK faces a range of terrorist threats. Groups may try to recruit people to their cause. Everyone in the UK should feel safe from this kind of extremism.

If you think someone is trying to persuade you to join an extremist or terrorist cause, you should notify your local police force.

Find out ...

✓ What is the role of the police?

✓ How are the police organised?

✓ What do Police and Crime Commissioners do and how are they selected?

✓ What do police community support officers do?

✓ How do you complain about the actions of the police?

✓ What sort of terrorist or extremist threats may occur in the UK?

✓ What should you do if you encounter any threat?

The role of the courts

The judiciary

Parliament makes law but judges are responsible for interpreting it and the government cannot interfere with this. If judges find a law to be illegal, the government must change it.

Judges also decide on disputes between people and organisations, and award compensation to whoever has suffered a loss. They do not decide whether people are guilty of crimes. This is the work of juries or magistrates. However, judges decide on the sentence given to serious offenders.

Criminal courts

Dealing with less serious offences

The Magistrates' Court (or a Justice of the Peace Court in Scotland) deals with minor offences. Magistrates hear cases in these courts. They are members of the local community and usually work unpaid. They receive training but do not need legal qualifications. Magistrates decide the verdict and the sentence if the defendant is found guilty.

In Northern Ireland, cases are heard by a District Judge or Deputy District Judge, who is legally qualified and paid.

Dealing with more serious offences

In England, Wales and Northern Ireland, cases are tried in front of a judge and a jury in a Crown Court. In Scotland cases are tried in a Sheriff Court with either a sheriff or a sheriff with a jury. The most serious cases in Scotland, such as murder, are heard at a High Court with a judge and jury.

Juries are chosen at random from the electoral register. Everyone must do jury service when asked unless they have a very good reason to be excused, such as ill health. The jury decides the verdict but the judge decides the penalty.

In Scotland 15 people sit on a jury. In England, Wales and Northern Ireland it is 12 people.

Dealing with young people

In England, Wales and Northern Ireland, some magistrates and District Judges are specially trained to work in the Youth Courts, which deal with young people aged between 10 and 17. Members of the public are not allowed in Youth Courts, and the young person's name cannot be published. Serious cases go to a Crown Court.

Parents or carers of the young person are expected to attend the hearing.

Find out …

✓ What is the system of youth justice in Scotland?

Civil courts

Many civil disputes are dealt with in the County Courts. These include recovering debts, personal injury and family matters, including divorce. In Scotland, most of these cases are dealt with in the Sheriff Court and more serious civil cases are dealt with in the Court of Session in Edinburgh.

When claims are small there is a different system. It is much cheaper because it does not involve solicitors. People sit round a table with a judge, who decides the case. There is also an online version of the small claims procedure.

Find out ...

✓ What sort of disputes do County Courts deal with?

✓ What is a small claims procedure?

Legal advice

Solicitors

Solicitors are trained in law and give advice on legal matters and represent their clients in court.

You can find solicitors all over the UK, but make sure that you use one with the expertise you need as many specialise in different areas. Before a solicitor starts on your case, ask how much it will cost.

Find out ...

✓ What do solicitors do?

✓ How can you find a solicitor?

Fundamental principles

Britain respects the individual's rights and ensures essential freedoms. These rights are incorporated into the European Convention on Human Rights and Fundamental Freedoms, also known as the European Convention on Human Rights. The UK was one of the first countries to sign the Convention in 1950.

The Human Rights Act 1998 incorporated the European Convention on Human Rights into UK law. The government, public bodies and the courts must follow the principles of the Convention.

Find out …

✓ How have rights and freedoms developed in the UK?

✓ What are the main features of the European Convention on Human Rights?

✓ How does the European Convention on Human Rights affect the UK?

Equal opportunities

UK laws ensure that people are not treated unfairly in any area of life or work because of their age, disability, sex, pregnancy and maternity, race, religion or belief, sexuality or marital status. If you face problems with discrimination, you should obtain advice.

Domestic violence

Violence towards a partner is a serious offence. For example, a man who forces a woman, including his wife, to have sex can be charged with rape.

Female genital mutilation

Female genital mutilation (FGM), also known as cutting or female circumcision, is illegal in the UK. Practising FGM or taking a girl abroad for FGM is a criminal offence.

Forced marriage

Forced marriage, where one or both people involved do not give their consent, is illegal in the UK. A court order can be taken out to prevent the marriage taking place. Anyone who breaches this order can go to prison for two years.

Find out ...

✓ What laws prevent forced marriage?

✓ Where can you go for advice if you have problems about equal opportunities?

✓ Where can you get help if you are subjected to domestic violence?

Taxation

People in the UK have to pay tax on their income. The money raised pays for government services such as roads, education, police and the armed forces.

Income tax is usually taken directly from your pay by your employer. If you are self-employed, you must pay your own tax through the 'self-assessment' system. Sometimes you are sent a tax return asking about your income. You must fill it in honestly and return it.

Almost everyone who is working must also pay National Insurance Contributions. These contributions are usually deducted the same way as income tax. Self-employed people must pay it themselves. If you do not make these payments you may not be able to claim benefits or receive a pension.

Every UK citizen is sent a National Insurance number as they approach 16. If you have permission to work in the UK, you should apply to the Department for Work and Pensions (DWP) for a number. You will need proof of identity and evidence that you are allowed to work. You can start work without a number, but you must apply for one.

Find out ...

✓ What does 'income' include?

✓ How are taxes paid in the UK?

✓ How does self-assessment work?

✓ What benefits are affected if you do not pay National Insurance?

Driving

You usually need to be at least 17 years old to drive a car or motorcycle. Different rules apply for commercial vehicles.

You must pass a test and get a licence. After the age of 70, your licence must be renewed every three years. People with an EU licence can drive until it runs out. There are different rules for people with other licences.

Your car must be insured unless it is off the road and not being driven. There are large fines for driving an uninsured car.

You must have paid vehicle tax. If you have not paid, your vehicle may be clamped or towed away.

Cars over three years old must have an MOT every year.

Find out ...

✓ How old do you have to be to drive different types of vehicle?

✓ What is an 'R' plate?

✓ What are the rules for people with overseas driving licences from outside the EU?

✓ How do you apply for vehicle tax?

✓ What does MOT stand for?

✓ Where can you find more information about vehicle taxation and MOTs?

Your role in the community

Values and responsibilities

Help and protect your family

Obey and respect the law

Behave responsibly

Help others

Respect and preserve the environment

Behave morally and ethically

Vote in local and national government elections

Treat others with fairness and respect

Work to provide for yourself

Treat everyone equally, regardless of sex, race, religion, age, disability, class or sexual orientation

These are some of the values shared by people who live in the UK. They make it easier to live together in a community.

Being a good neighbour

When you move into a neighbourhood, introduce yourself to the people living nearby. Getting on with the neighbours always makes life easier.

There are all sorts of activities going on in most communities. The people who run them often want others to help. By joining in, you get to know more people and become part of the community.

Find out ...

✓ How can you prevent conflict with your neighbours?

How you can support your community

Jury service

People who have the right to vote may be asked to serve on a jury. People are selected at random from the electoral register to decide the verdict in more serious criminal trials.

Find out ...

✓ How old must you be to serve on a jury?

Helping in schools

Schools often like parents to help by listening to children reading or supporting classroom activities. You can find out about such opportunities by asking in school or reading newsletters that children bring home. Most schools have a parent–teacher association (PTA). PTAs often organise fund-raising events and need helpers. This is a good way to get to know people in the community.

Parents and other community groups in England can set up a state-funded free school if there is a local need. More information can be found at www.dfe.gov.uk, the website of the Department for Education.

School governors (school boards in Scotland) play an important part in raising school standards. They have three key roles:

- setting the strategic direction of the school
- ensuring accountability
- monitoring and evaluating school performance.

You can contact your local school to ask if they need a new governor or school board member. In England, you can also apply online at the School Governors' One-Stop Shop at www.sgoss.org.uk.

Find out …

✓ How can you help in school?

✓ Where can you find further information on becoming a governor or school board member?

Political parties

You can join the political party which matches your views. As a result you will be involved in the democratic process. Parties always want help at election time because members go 'canvassing', which includes knocking on people's doors to ask for support. You don't have to tell a canvasser your views if you don't want to.

If you wish to become even more involved you can stand for office as a local councillor, member of Parliament or member of the European Parliament.

You can find out more about joining a political party from the individual party websites.

Find out ...

✓ How do you join a political party?

✓ What is 'the democratic process'?

Local services

There are other ways to support local services in your community, for example, as:

- a special constable or lay representative with the police
- a magistrate.

You can find out more about these sorts of roles at www.gov.uk.

Blood and organ donation

Both blood and organs can be donated to help other people.

You can find out more about donating blood at the following websites:

- England and North Wales: www.blood.co.uk
- Rest of Wales: www.welsh-blood.org.uk
- Scotland: www.scotblood.co.uk
- Northern Ireland: www.nibts.org

To find out more about organ donation, go to www.organdonation.nhs.uk

Volunteering

Volunteers work for a good causes without payment. This not only helps the local or national organisation, but also the individual volunteer. You get to know people and develop skills that may be useful when looking for a job.

There are many different volunteer roles. Some people help in local hospitals – for example, by running a shop or coffee shop for visitors or just helping people to find their way about. There are organisations which help the homeless. There are also many volunteer roles with the National Trust, which is a nationwide organisation that looks after stately homes and historic monuments.

Whatever your interest, there will be an organisation which would like your help.

Find out …

✓ Where can you find information about charities and other organisations that might be looking for volunteers?

Looking after the environment

Looking after the environment is important in every community. All local councils have systems to help you recycle your waste. This reduces the amount of waste that goes into landfill.

It also helps if you shop locally and walk or use public transport as much as possible.

Find out …

✓ What are the main benefits of recycling?

✓ How is household waste recycled in your local area?

Practice questions

Question 1   Is the statement below ☐ TRUE or ☐ FALSE?

Democracy is a system of government where the people elect their representatives to make decisions on their behalf.

Question 2   Which TWO values and responsibilities should you have as a UK citizen or permanent resident?

☐ **A**   To vote in local and national elections
☐ **B**   To treat everyone equally
☐ **C**   To have religious beliefs
☐ **D**   To have lots of noisy house parties

Question 3   Which of the following statements is correct?

☐ **A**   The cabinet is made up of ministers in charge of government departments.
☐ **B**   The cabinet is made up of the newest members of Parliament.

Question 4   What other group supports the police in their work?

☐ **A**   Police community support officers
☐ **B**   Public community safety officers
☐ **C**   Police central support officials
☐ **D**   Public control support officials

Question 5   Is the statement below ☐ TRUE or ☐ FALSE?

You can smoke tobacco wherever you like in the UK.

Question 6 Which of the following statements is correct?

☐ **A** The Foreign Secretary is responsible for immigration.

☐ **B** The Foreign Secretary is responsible for managing relationships with foreign countries.

Question 7 What does money raised from income tax pay for?

☐ **A** The BBC

☐ **B** The National Trust

☐ **C** Government services

☐ **D** Social networking

Question 8 Who is head of state in the United Kingdom?

☐ **A** The Prime Minister

☐ **B** The Archbishop of Canterbury

☐ **C** The Lord Chancellor

☐ **D** The monarch

Question 9 Which of the following statements is correct?

☐ **A** In a Crown Court case the judge decides the sentence when someone is found guilty.

☐ **B** In a Crown Court case the jury decides the sentence when someone is found guilty.

Question 10 What is the area called that is represented by a member of Parliament?

☐ **A** State

☐ **B** Council

☐ **C** Constituency

☐ **D** Ward

Question 11 Who can become a school governor or a member of the school board?

☐ **A** Only parents who have a child at the school

☐ **B** People from the local community

☐ **C** Past students and teachers who are familiar with the school

☐ **D** Local council members

Question 12 Is the statement below ☐ TRUE or ☐ FALSE?

The British constitution is written down in a single document.

Question 13 Which of the following statements is correct?

☐ **A** A government made up of members from more than one party is called a minority government.

☐ **B** A government made up of members from more than one party is called a coalition government.

Question 14 Is the statement below ☐ TRUE or ☐ FALSE?

If you have not paid sufficient National Insurance Contributions you will not be entitled to some state benefits.

Question 15 Which TWO areas of life are protected by equality legislation?

☐ **A** Choice of clothing

☐ **B** Where you live

☐ **C** Race

☐ **D** Sexuality

Question 16 Which of the following statements is correct?

☐ **A** The powers of the Welsh Assembly include defence and foreign affairs.

☐ **B** The powers of the Welsh Assembly include economic development.

Question 17 A Ministry of Transport (MOT) certificate is required for every car that is over how many years old?

☐ **A** 1

☐ **B** 3

☐ **C** 7

☐ **D** 5

Question 18 Is the statement below ☐ TRUE or ☐ FALSE?

The civil service is politically neutral.

Question 19 Which of the following statements is correct?

☐ **A** You can vote in elections in person at a polling station or through a postal ballot.

☐ **B** You can only vote in elections at a polling station.

Question 20 What is the second-largest party in the House of Commons usually called?

☐ **A** Minority party

☐ **B** Challenging party

☐ **C** The other side

☐ **D** The opposition

Answers and pointers to questions

Question	Answer	Explanation	Page reference in *Life in the United Kingdom: A Guide for New Residents*
1	TRUE	Democracy is a system of government where the whole adult population gets a say. This might be by direct voting or by choosing representatives to make decisions on their behalf.	Page 119
2	A and B	In the UK there is a set of shared values and responsibilities that everyone can agree with. These include voting in local and national elections, and treating everyone equally.	Page 154
3	A	The Prime Minister appoints about 20 senior MPs to become ministers in charge of departments. These ministers form a cabinet, a committee which usually meets weekly and makes important decisions about government policy.	Page 127
4	A	Police officers are supported by police community support officers (PCSOs). PCSOs usually patrol the streets, support police officers at crime scenes and major events, and work with the public.	Pages 142–3
5	FALSE	It is against the law to smoke tobacco products in nearly every enclosed public place in the UK. There are signs displayed to tell you where you cannot smoke.	Page 141
6	B	The Foreign Secretary is responsible for managing relationships with foreign countries, and is a member of the cabinet.	Page 127

Question	Answer	Explanation	Page reference in *Life in the United Kingdom: A Guide for New Residents*
7	C	Money raised from income tax pays for government services such as roads, education, police and the armed forces.	Page 151
8	D	The monarch is head of state in the UK. The current monarch is Queen Elizabeth II.	Page 121
9	A	In a Crown Court the jury listens to the evidence presented at the trial and then decides on a verdict of 'guilty' or 'not guilty'. If the jury finds a defendant guilty, the judge decides on the sentence.	Pages 145–6
10	C	The UK is divided into parliamentary constituencies. Voters in each constituency elect their member of Parliament (MP) in a General Election.	Page 123
11	B	School governors, or members of the school board in Scotland, are people from the local community who wish to make a positive contribution to children's education.	Page 156
12	FALSE	The British constitution is not written down in any single document, and therefore it is described as 'unwritten'.	Page 120
13	B	If one party does not get a majority vote at a General Election, two or more parties can join together to form a coalition.	Page 123
14	TRUE	Anyone who does not pay enough National Insurance Contributions will not be able to receive certain contributory benefits, such as Jobseeker's Allowance or a full state retirement pension.	Page 151

Question	Answer	Explanation	Page reference in *Life in the United Kingdom: A Guide for New Residents*
15	C and D	There are laws to ensure that people are not treated unfairly in any area of work or life because of their disability, marital status, age, pregnancy and maternity, sex, race, religion or belief, or sexuality.	Page 149
16	B	The Welsh Assembly has the power to make laws for Wales in many areas, including economic development, health and social services, housing and education. Defence and foreign affairs remain under central UK government control.	Pages 129–30
17	B	If your car is over three years old, you must take it for a Ministry of Transport (MOT) test every year. (If your car is new, it will need an MOT test after three years, and then every year.)	Page 153
18	TRUE	Civil servants in the UK are politically neutral, and are not political appointees.	Pages 128–9
19	A	People vote in elections at polling stations (polling places in Scotland). If it is difficult for you to get to a polling station or polling place, you can register for a postal ballot.	Page 135
20	D	The second-largest party in the House of Commons is usually called the opposition.	Page 127